Praise For Overcoming Emotic

"...I have fostered over 40 teen boys since 1994 and with my wife, have adopted five children who have experienced great trauma in their lives. I wish this book had been available 30 years ago as I negotiated a world of pain and hurt carried around by my clients and those coming to my home."

~ Mr. Kim Combes, M.Ed
Counselor, Adoptive Parent,
Writer and National Presenter

"Travis's ability to connect trauma 'theory' to 'reality' is accurately mesmerizing. This book is a learning tool that will change the face of trauma training in America!"

~Helen Hall Ramaglia
"The Trauma Queen"
Abuse, Foster Care & Trauma Survivor,
National Speaker

"He is able to see past the idea of "trauma informed" to the practice of trauma informed. He makes the solutions to recovering from trauma practical and doable. He is not speaking from theory but speaking from his heart because he has walked the road himself. He is exceptional in his determination to not only change his own perspective but use his experience and knowledge to help change the world!"

~Christy Meyer
Retired Therapist, Nebraska/Iowa

Excellent insight provided about a very challenging subject faced by helping professionals. Travis always brings a warm and humanistic approach to his work as a public speaker and now has been able to translate this in to his writing. A useful tool for those of us who wish to create a better future and better outcomes for youth aging out of foster care.

~Valerie Welsh
Social Worker, Las Vegas, NV

OVERCOMING EMOTIONAL TRAUMA

LIFE BEYOND SURVIVAL MODE

TRAVIS LLOYD

Published And Printed In The United States Of America

For information on bulk order discounts contact
Changing Lives Entertainment, LLC
www.ChangingLivesEntertainment.com
(646) 535-8728

First Edition November 2014

Book Cover Design By Silvana Bossa
Layout Design By Silvana Bossa
Copy Editing And Revisions By Laura McClelland
Additional Copy Editing By Dr. John Degarmo

While the author has made every effort to provide accurate web addresses or other
informations at the time of publication, neither the publisher nor the author assumes
any responsibility for errors, or for changes that occur after publication. Neither the
author nor publisher has any control over and does not recommend, endorse or assume
responsibility for third-party services, products, websites or their content.

Dates, names, locations, and other potentially identifying information related to any stories
in this book may have been changed to protect the identity of sensitive information.

CONTENTS

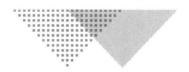

FOREWORD

by Dr. Chris Downs

There are as many stories about living in substitute care systems (foster care, juvenile corrections, runaway and homeless shelters, mental health facilities, residential care homes) as there are children who have lived in those systems. No two stories are alike.

Youth enter and leave these systems at different ages, developmental stages, and for a host of reasons. In my case, at only an hour old I was taken from my birth mother and immediately placed into the care of the State of Indiana. A final adoption wasn't in the cards for nearly two years. Other children spend a lot of time with their birth families, but for a host of reasons they leave those families and enter substitute care. Still others get pushed away from their families while others flee similar families to avoid abuse and torment.

On the other side of these systems is the concept of "exit" from care. I've spent many years working with substitute care systems and rarely see an "exit" that reminds me of one I've witnessed before. Whether an adoption at age 2, reunification with one's original family at age 7, a kinship guardianship at age 9, or "emancipation" when the state will no longer provide care (at age 18 or 23 or whenever), exits never seem to look alike either.

For professionals like me who like clean, crisp categories of people, places, and events, the ebb and flow of children into and out of substitute systems are challenging. Over the many years I've studied in this area, it's clear that, in general, children come into the care of the system for these reasons:

neglect from their parents, emotional abuse and trauma, sexual and physical abuse – usually from parents, or because they are separated from their families because (1) they just don't fit there anymore, (2) because the families don't want them, or (3) the parent(s) die.

If the concept of a family not wanting a child is difficult for you, I'm glad. It's a concept with which we should all struggle. That said, it happens all the time. Parents give up newborns, boys who too often play with dolls, girls who too often play with trucks, autistic children, behaviorally disruptive children, LGBTQ youth, kids doing drugs, and "defiant" children and they give them up every single day in America. If any of these surprise you, good. Perhaps you need to be surprised. A little surprise mixed with anger would be just about right.

Young people come into substitute care at all ages and for a host of reasons that may surprise and anger us. You may know all of this. But did you also know that the older the age of the child entering the system, the harder it is for them to get back out of the system? In fact, the average age of youth in foster care is over 10. As a rule of thumb, I've found that if a child comes into substitute care at age 8 or later, they will have a much harder time getting back to a safe, stable, loving home compared with younger children.

There are just as many stories about how young people exit care. However, their stories can generally be classified into five types. First are those infants, children, and adolescents who stay only for a relatively short time and return home or to other family members, such as aunts, uncles, grandparents, cousins, and so on. These are generally the lucky ones who avoid long stays in substitute care.

Second are youth who die in or shortly after they leave care. Some of the reasons they die are expected: illness, the medically fragile state of their bodies, trauma, or other factors making it likely that they won't survive. In rare cases, the trauma they experience in care causes death or they are killed by their caregivers. These frequently hit the evening news and cause tons of (usually well-deserved) public outcry.

Third are the "failures" we read about so often in the media; these are the young people who "graduate" from care to homelessness, adult corrections, poverty, and other undesirable outcomes. Research conducted by my colleagues and I and separately by Mark Courtney and others demonstrate that the road out of substitute care is often lonely, scary, unsupported, and daunting. Up to 50% of youth who "emancipate" from substitute care are homeless, at least temporarily, during the first six months after they leave care. These youth are more likely to be arrested, be unemployed or underemployed as young adults, less likely to have successful relationships, and achieve lower incomes as adults.

Fourth are the vast numbers of alumni of care about whom we have little or no information. State welfare systems have not done a very good job tracking where youth go, how they fare, and so forth. These are the alumni we just don't know about. I recall talking with a recently emancipated foster youth who told me she wouldn't talk with a social worker about her experience in care if her life depended on it. It was just too painful for her and she wanted to move on with her life.

Finally, is the group of alumni of care who succeed despite all odds. These are the people who overcome obstacles, decide that no matter the challenge it can be met, and who are often described as "resilient." These are the "Rocky" type adults coming out of the juvenile corrections, mental health, and foster care systems. They have been knocked down over and over again, only to rise and take on the next challenge.

You are about to read a book about just such a person, a "Rocky." This is a person who didn't die in or right after care.

He didn't graduate into any of the terrible institutions that are the homes for many who emancipate from care. And while he could have been one of the vast number of adults who never spoke up about his experiences, he decided that he would share his story, if only to improve the possible outcome of even one child or adolescent in care.

Travis Lloyd's story is one of resiliency, well-informed decision-making, and a never-give-up spirit. It's also a story about the identification of supporters (some call them Elders or Mentors) who could offer guidance along the way. His is a story that offers many lessons for youth struggling to come to grips with some very basic, existential questions such as: "Why am I here?" "Why has God decided to punish me by putting me into foster care?" "When can I finally have a home?" "Why isn't my Mom like other moms?" "When will I ever get a break?"

I've known Travis for years. I've seen him struggle, survive, and thrive. His is a story worth knowing. My hope is that by reading this book you will find several ways you can be a part of the success of young people still in substitute care systems or perhaps even offer help to those who have recently come out of such systems. Travis will identify so many ways that you can support changes and improvements to an individual, a group of youth, or even to systems reform.

For those of you who may still be on your journey of overcoming and seeking your path in life, you too will gain a great deal of insight and inspiration to aid you in your journey. Regardless of your personal or professional background, Travis' stories will inspire and empower.

The words in this book give a recognizable, human face to stories we might hear about, but discount because it seems too foreign or strange for someone who may have had a stable upbringing. Statistics on a page can only affect you so much. Statistics on a page do not come close to reading about a child in a group home, crying for a mother he hasn't seen in months, or how trapped someone feels as they stare up at their bedroom ceiling at night listening to their parents scream at each other. The combination of real, visceral (and oftentimes, funny) autobiography mixed with advice provides added weight to what Travis will share with you. Gandhi advised us all to "be a part of the change you want to see." The advice Travis shares has worked for him; his words might be just what you need to inspire change and healing in your own life, and those around you as well.

Overcoming Emotional Trauma
Life Beyond Survival Mode

It means the world to me that you have decided to give this book a small amount of your time and attention. Since you've made it this far, I would like to kindly ask you to leave a review on Amazon. As a first time author, your feedback very significantly impacts the likelihood of someone choosing to read this book and develop their own emotional wellness. Please help them see the power in this message that I believe in with all of my heart. You can leave feedback by finding this book on Amazon and logging in or you may follow this link to Amazon:

http://bit.ly/OvercomingEmotionalTrauma

Thank you!

TRAVIS LLOYD

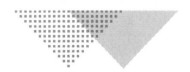

PROLOGUE

There are millions of people with horrific stories much worse than mine. These people often don't have a voice and feel completely alone. I once felt voiceless, but along this never-ending journey, I have been blessed with the ability to write, speak, and use my voice in a way that many are still afraid to do. Therefore, I strive to help them know they are not alone, through sharing my story in a way that I hope will inspire, educate, and empower.

Throughout this book, I will be sharing details of personal experiences, both as a mental health professional and former foster youth. I have spoken about some of these stories in my presentations to thousands of foster youth, homeless youth, foster parents, college students and child welfare professionals all across the United States. Sometimes I felt like I was on top of the world and just knew that I had blown the entire audience away. Other times, I felt like I completely bombed the speech, and wondered why in the world I was ever there to begin with. Regardless, something cool happened every single time. There was always at least one brave soul that approached me to share that hearing about my triumphs helped them build the courage to start working towards their own. This handful of people has inspired me to continue following my dreams as a speaker and performer. Along with this, they inspired me to write these stories and insights about overcoming emotional trauma to live a happier, healthier and more successful life.

Some people hear a traumatic childhood story and think, "Oh my gosh! I could never imagine such horror!" My goal for this book is not to offer a sob story about a rough childhood or seek approval for accomplishments. Instead, the goal is to relate to both sides while also entertaining and inspiring an expanded insight to the adults, professionals, and mentors who work with those who have experienced both large traumatic events as well as on-going smaller events. When you read about some of my personal testimonies of overcoming adverse scenarios, it is my hope that you enjoy the stories while also reflecting on how you or someone you know may be able to relate to, learn, and grow from the outcomes. These lessons may be exactly what you need, and to inspire you to improve your life. At the same time, there might also be something that is exactly what you are meant to share with a loved one, friend, co-worker, or client.

These stories will provide an opportunity for you to relate to real life experiences while also serving as learning points. I will share with you the practical ways that I was able to overcome emotional trauma, foster care, group homes, and break generational curses not only for myself, but also my family.

Here is what you can expect:

- Real life stories that may shock you
- To be entertained while addressing many topics such as foster care, group homes, drugs, human services, trauma, and emotional barriers to growth
- A clinical viewpoint of some of these stories from a professional psychologist
- An easy-to-read conversation form of writing
- Stories and advice that provide both as inspiration and guidance for self-help
- Autobiographical stories of trauma to educate, empower and enlighten while offering insight into difficulties that millions still struggle with, but few talk about or overcome

Do Not Expect:

- My stories or opinions to be politically correct
- Sob stories or the vibe of "The Lost Child"
- A formal "How to improve your life" book - there is no one-size-fits-all, but if you or someone you know can relate to my story it will push you in the right direction for personal growth
- To relate to my story - even if you are from Venus and I am from Mars; you will likely still be entertained or understand more about someone in your personal or professional life

Everyone has a journey, and the most important thing is that we continue to learn along our individual paths. My journey has taught me to understand the various paths that others have taken who have not experienced a life in survival mode. My career has taught me empathy and compassion. Fortunately, I have friends and family who have reminded me that not everyone is capable of "toughing it out" the way that I have learned to do. Therefore, I feel it necessary to state that, in general, I am very compassionate and believe in unconditional love, personal awareness, growth, and helping others. In fact, I have realized that the only time I feel like I am truly serving my purpose is when I'm serving others. That is also one of the main reasons why I started writing this book. It is my hope that the stories, thoughts, and insight shared in this book touch you, and many more lives than I could imagine.

CHAPTER 1

INTRODUCTION

"...I share this brief bio and list of accomplishments with you not to brag, but to point out that I was once told that I was more likely to be dead or in jail by the age of 18."

Any given event in a person's life can be considered "traumatic," depending on the individual's perception. This means that two people can experience the same exact situation, such as a car crash, and one of them can walk away just fine without the experience impacting their life or daily activities. Meanwhile, the other person may have seen their life flash before their eyes and be so traumatized that they call in to work sick the next day, as they spiral down into a deep depression.

There are many things in life that impact how you will react to any potentially stressful situation. How you were raised, the amount of affection you received, whether or not you have felt overwhelmed in previous similar situations, what you fear, and how much of a support system you currently have are just a few of the things that impact your reactions. To be sure, no two people's experiences are the same. I'm different, you're different, and the weird lady walking her cat down the street on a leash is different, as well. We each react differently when overwhelmed, and that's okay. But what I don't think is okay is living life without understanding the experiences that shape our current lives and interactions with others. I lived like that for much of my life, and finally reached a point where I decided it was time to overcome my past and live happier!

This realization meant I had a lot of internal work to do. I also discovered that the internal work never ends. After a while, it becomes habit, and makes it seem a lot less like work and a lot more like life; "normal" life. Once I started to overcome much of my past I was able to see — I mean truly see — what "normal" felt and looked like in the lives of people who emitted happiness. I don't mean those who seem happy on the outside, because they have everything they need or want. Instead, I mean those people who truly have a light shining from their soul that reflects on those around them. It's not something that can be easily described, but you know it when you feel it. It's like that wise old man who looks you in the eyes, and without saying a word, tells you he sees through your lies and understands why you are lying, at the same time wishing better for you. It's that nice co-worker who watches you completely screw something up, and instead of mocking you, gives you a kind smile and helping hand while gently explaining how to avoid similar mishaps in the future before anyone else might notice. Having lived most of my life not understanding how people could do such a thing as react positively in negative situations, it took me a long time to realize that those simple gestures indicate the presence of one very powerful term: emotional intelligence.

Emotional intelligence is the ability to monitor your own emotions while being aware of the emotions that others are likely experiencing in the same moment. It helps you identify different emotions and be able to describe them appropriately. You can then use emotional information to guide the way you think and act (or react).

Becoming aware of this term and what it looked like in my own life helped me develop and practice emotional intelligence. After finding this emotional intelligence in myself, I began noticing that many others around me had yet to find it. I noticed that a lot of people lack emotional intelligence. People from all walks of life; poor, rich, educated, middle school drop-outs, politicians, janitors, principals, teachers, therapists; the list goes on. One common thing that I found when interacting with each of them is that the biggest barrier to living a happier life with emotional intelligence is the fear of overcoming emotional trauma. Emotional trauma is characterized by many fears.

It is the fear of success that causes self-sabotage because you're not sure if you'll be able to handle the responsibility of making your dreams come true. It is the fear of intimacy that causes you to feel like you are living a double life in all romantic relationships. It is the fear that somewhere in your soul lies the answer to overcoming all of your fears to simply live happier. It is the fear that someday your past experiences, or negative behaviors, might creep up at the wrong time and ruin everything you've worked for. This fear is so crippling that you might fight to hold on to everything that you aren't actually happy with. Being so afraid to lose who you think you are prevents you from being everything you are meant to be. You might be there yourself at this time; in a state of self-sabotage that is easily justified and not easily recognized. If you are, I promise that you know at least a few people who are also there. I know; I have been there, myself. In my opinion, when you are not quite ready to accept that there have most likely been some events in your life that you perceived as traumatic, then you might dismiss this topic as insignificant. I urge you to reconsider.

If you are reading this as someone who simply does not relate to what is often viewed as "traumatic events," then I encourage you to consider the following story. Imagine a sixteen year old neighbor girl who simply gets under your skin. She annoys you with cursing, loud music, and her friends' cars sitting out front of your home when she sneaks out at all hours of the night. Your first instinct might be to assume how much she "gets around" or is simply a "bad kid." Can you be empathetic rather than pitifully sympathetic, or even spiteful? Will you be able to look beyond her facade and say the right encouraging words she needs, rather than give her a dirty look and hope you don't have to talk to her? Or will you respond instead in a condescending manner and place judgment, adding one more negative memory to her already tarnished soul? There is always reason behind behavior, and you never know what someone might be going through in their own world. That same 16 year old girl might be someone who was dealing with very significant emotional trauma, such as early childhood sexual abuse, incest, or drug addiction. Due to my experience working in inpatient psychiatric units, a pediatric emergency department, and as a community based mental health crisis worker, I can assure you that these examples are much more common, in even your neighborhood, than most people can imagine.

If you have had an "easy" life where you never had to worry about much and you were always taken care of, I challenge you to look at less obvious things. What about how your parents spoke to you? Did you always have to try and live up to their expectations only to be knocked down with statements like, "You could do better" or "I expected more"? Little subliminal things that knock down our self-esteem over time can also be very traumatic and shape the way we view the world and react in stressful situations. This applies to all relationships, including in the workplace.

If, on the other hand, you have been through a lot and often see what others go through and respond in your own head by saying, "I have been through worse; if only they knew," then I challenge you to search for a deeper understanding of your reaction. Are you re-living your struggles rather than being empathetic towards others? Are you always comparing your own life to others, or justifying negative behaviors with a traumatic childhood as the "reason" to continue a specific behavior that you know just doesn't feel right?

Keep in mind that negative behaviors could be as subtle as consistently talking badly about a co-worker, or as serious as drug use, avoiding one's emotions, or infidelity. If you fall under these categories or anything in-between, you might find that you are preventing yourself from living a fulfilling life and, even worse, unintentionally hurting those around you.

If you are a caregiver or professional in a helping field, I hope that these stories re-inspire your efforts and remind you why you do what you do. It is very easy to get accustomed to a routine process with policies and procedures, and sometimes we forget to see the people through the situation. Every person, no matter their education or socioeconomic status, has hopes, dreams, wants and needs; this includes you. Remember that you are human, too, and taking care of your own needs is important so that you can be your best for those in need.

I offer insight and inspiration to anyone who seeks personal growth and happiness. The following is a list of clearly identified audiences that will help you identify how to immediately apply this book to your personal or professional life.

Teachers/Educators - Not only are you charged with the responsibility of educating our youth, you also have the opportunity to help them grow emotionally. Just one word from you can change the life of a young person if you are able to identify their symptoms of emotional trauma and offer support, caring guidance, and appropriate referrals. Believe it or not, pills aren't the catch-all fix for disruptive classroom behaviors. Developing a bond and showing that you care as a person, not just as a teacher, can go much further than a trip to the nurse's office for a cup full of pills.

Foster & Adoptive Youth (current & former)
- It is well known that most of us struggle with abandonment, abuse, neglect and attachment issues. For those who might not be familiar with this phenomenon, here are a few stats originally published by Casey Family Programs:

"The prevalence of lifetime PTSD was significantly higher among alumni (30.0%) than among the general population (7.6%). This lifetime PTSD rate was comparable to that of Vietnam War veterans (30.9% for male veterans and 26.9% for female veterans)" (109)

-One in four alumni (25.2%) experienced PTSD within the previous 12 months (of the study)." "The prevalence of mental, emotional, and behavioral disorders among alumni (of foster care) exceeded that of the general population on all nine mental, emotional, and behavioral disorders that were assessed" (109).

These are all common side effects of childhood trauma that interfere with our ability to maintain important relationships in our lives and just feel "normal." Know that you are not alone, and that no matter what anyone has told you, there is a way to live your best life and be happy. It's a rough road, but I want to help you get there. The Alumni Studies Report was co-authored by Dr. Chris Downs, my good friend and colleague who provided the forward for this book.

Foster & Adoptive Parents - Your love, guidance, and compassion provides the hope that our young people need. Studies have shown that a young person's brain does not fully develop until their mid-twenties. If you make a commitment to a child, stick it out and support them as much as possible, within reason, even after age 18, or whatever age your state ends financial support for foster youth. Going through the transition to adulthood is tough enough for any youth with a "normal" family. Losing the only surrogate family they may know puts them at a much higher risk for drug use, depression, suicide, and prison. Their behaviors may worsen, especially at this age. Yet, everyone needs to feel unconditional love and acceptance, even if it comes with strict boundaries. Remember that there is so much more to these young people than meets the eye. They may not be emotionally the same as your biological child. They need to be understood, guided firmly, and most importantly, loved unconditionally. No matter how smart you are or what degree or level of life experience you have, these relationships often benefit from counseling. If you're dealing with a tough child, try seeking counseling for yourself to better understand his behavior before "quitting" on them. Heck, you can even write me and I would be happy to talk with you. If you were to want to quit on anyone, it would have been me at the age of 18. As you will soon read, I had a very rough transition. This transition of mine was one that was facilitated by unconditional and tough love from someone who cared enough to not give up on me.

Health Care Professionals - If there is one thing that my ten plus years of experience has taught me about the health care industry, it is that my fellow health care providers are natural caretakers of others, but often fail to tend to our own needs. In general, this is assumed to be physical needs such as healthy eating and exercise. Although this is true, I have observed that a lack of tending to emotional health is even more prominent. Before we are able to give our patients what they need, and guide them appropriately, we must address our own "issues." No matter how hard you might try, stuffing it all away inevitably shows in how you care for patients. Later I will share about the moment when I learned the true meaning of treating a patient as a person, rather than as a job. It is amazing how transparent a nurse or doctor is when they stop treating their patients as people, just to avoid experiencing their own feelings. This goes for everyone in health care settings; the registration clerks, dietary aids, respiratory therapists, etc. Anyone in a helping profession benefits from this reminder: Deal with your own "issues," and you will better connect with ~~patients~~ people.

Oh, and by the way, I'm a Registered Nurse with experience in hospital emergency departments, caring for sick and injured youth and adults, as well as previous experience in inpatient mental health services. Both settings address an abundance of social service issues related to traumatizing experiences, from medical trauma to child and spousal abuse. I am most passionate about crisis intervention. This passion stems from the same reason that I am writing this book, because I feel called to use my stories and experience to help others overcome mentally and emotionally disturbing situations. While writing a portion of this book, I maintained an active role as a mental health mobile crisis worker with law enforcement across two counties, including one metropolitan area. Crisis workers in this role report to the scene where a crisis has occurred, along-side police officers. The most recognizable examples of such situations are when officers need a crisis worker to "talk a guy off the bridge," or intervene when a schizophrenic is demonstrating psychotic behaviors that are disturbing the public. Other common situations included behavioral problems in schools and homes that had escalated beyond the scope of the family or caretakers. I am also an adjunct professor, professional speaker, hip-hop artist, poet, actor, author, uncle, brother, son, and nephew. Prior to completing this book, I was accepted as a doctoral student.

I share this brief bio and list of accomplishments with you not to brag, but to point out that I was once told that I was more likely to be dead or in jail by the age of 18 than I was to graduate high school. The accomplishment of being accepted to a doctoral program is something that is achieved by less than 1% of those who have experienced living in foster care, for more than 30 days at a young age, such as myself. I think that this is pretty awesome. I also believe that each and every person deserves to feel supported and empowered to find their own awesomeness! To remind you of your awesomeness, I'd like to share with you a quote that I created during a time that I volunteered with foster youth: "No matter where you come from or where you want to go, it's possible." I encourage you to tweet that.

Due to improved self-awareness of my passion and purpose, I chose to postpone graduate studies to write, travel, and speak. Following my gut instinct to drop the program later proved to be a very wise decision that allowed me many experiences of a lifetime. I happened to write this introductory chapter while on an extended visit to Monterrey, Mexico, in between learning Spanish, taking salsa lessons and realizing that I still have a lot to learn about the world and other cultures. It was pretty amazing to experience first hand, how much your mind expands when exposed to different cultures and ways of simply living life. This would not have been possible had I not followed my gut instinct. With all this I call success, I feel very fortunate. Yet, I realize that not everyone is as fortunate, and I haven't always been, either.

Although I will forever battle with the remnants of my past, I have broken negative life cycles thought to be nearly impossible to break. If you or someone you know are stuck in a rut and desire a deeper level of happiness, I hope that the stories and insight offered in this book provide you with the necessary tools and inspiration to break your own negative cycles. Remember that success is not measured in the value of your home or belongings, but in the value of your self-worth, relationships and how you serve others.

It has been my experience that the "things" that you want, need, and desire will come when you incorporate this idea of value into your daily life. Being emotionally well is a prerequisite to being mentally, emotionally, and physically prepared to do what it takes to get where you want to go in life through relationships, talents and professional goals. I strive to inspire the internal motivation that it takes for you to break the mold in whatever real or perceived barriers you may face. If you have a friend, family member, co-worker or client who faces many emotional barriers, I hope to inspire you to have the strength, courage, determination and understanding to not give up on those who have been called hopeless, as I have myself.

It is not without fear, but with the desire of helping that I welcome you to the stories and lessons that have molded me into the person I am today. The initial portion of this book will offer a chronological history of the major traumatizing events in my childhood. You will receive clinical explanations of the impact of such traumas from Dr. Gregory Keck, a good friend and colleague who has been a long time supporter of my personal and professional development. He is also a leading international authority on relationship and attachment disorders related to traumatized youth, and the founding psychologist of The Attachment and Bonding Centers of Ohio. You will be able to review the timeline of my life, alongside that of another individual who was born the same year I was and has experienced many similar traumatizing experiences, but is now in prison. I believe this will provide a unique perspective that will allow you to observe the similarities and differences that propelled each of us to the lives that we now live. Dr. Keck will offer a brief analysis of both timelines. The remainder of the book will focus on sharing the tips and life lessons that have allowed me to overcome and live a happier and healthier life. Many of the stories utilized to reinforce these learning points will offer a more detailed understanding of significant events from the historical timeline of my life, later referred to as my "roadmap". The stories will not progress in chronological order, but instead will highlight important lessons that have allowed me and many others to overcome. So join me, and let's begin with where the need for healing most often first develops; childhood.

CHAPTER 2

INITIAL TRAUMA

"It was scary. The smells were odd. The people were odd. Nobody showed any affection..."

There are many people who could never imagine surviving the life that I lived as a child, teen, and young adult. On the other hand, I feel very fortunate because I can't count the number of people I have personally met who had a much worse childhood than I did. Allow me to correct myself; I can't count the number of people I have personally met who currently still have a life much worse than even I could ever imagine. Some people were never even lucky enough to have happy memories. I'm glad I did.

I remember my mother telling me about my fifth birthday. I woke up -rather early in the morning, wrapped a bath towel around my neck like Superman, and ran around the house screaming "I'm 5! I'm 5! I'm 5!" I was jumping off of furniture as if I could defy gravity, followed by the inevitable thump when I hit the ground. I was fearless, care-free and oh, by the way, I was completely naked!

I don't have many memories like this that bring a childish smile to my face. In fact, this was one of the last vivid memories that I recall before the care-free Travis seemed to disappear and memories were burned into my mind that still, to this day, cause tears to build. This emotional response to childhood memories is often seen as a weakness amongst the general public, or among those "manly men" that a boy might look up to, as I did. But the truth is that the childhood memories that have the ability to create such an emotional response are an indicator of emotional trauma. Some call this having Adverse Childhood Experiences (ACE). The most well-known documentation of ACE is the Adverse Childhood Experiences Study conducted by Kaiser Permanente Health Maintenance Organization and Centers for Disease Control and Prevention. This study is slowly being disseminated nation-wide from the federal level down to regional, state, and local mental health agencies. The goal of many organizations is to not just use the ACE Study to improve mental health services to the chronically mentally ill, but to bring a larger awareness of what a traumatizing experience is, and how it impacts adulthood. With a larger awareness of the root cause of poor mental wellness, communities can improve as a whole, rather than as individuals.

Critical Thinking Moment: When was the last time you felt that a supervisor or colleague was abusing their power, or an employee was not performing their best? Each of these situations often means there is an underlying issue. Finding ways to deal with those underlying issues in a caring way, that facilitates positive outcomes for all involved, is what the research from the ACE Study allows you to do. It improves relationships and even in corporate settings it improves outcomes and productivity.

I encourage you to spread awareness of the ACE Study to any organization that you are involved in or work with. A wealth of information is available to help you gain a deeper understanding of implementing trauma informed care practices at www. TraumaInformedCareProject.org.

The ACE Study essentially proves that even minor traumatic experiences can cause behavior changes and health problems throughout one's life-span, especially when left unaddressed. It even goes as far as to document undeniable correlations between negative childhood experiences and higher rates of diabetes, major depression, and even early death. To me, this study is the "red tape" data that allows government organizations to implement common sense into their federal and state guidelines for money allocations in mental health services. Although it may be obvious to some people that there is a direct correlation between a traumatizing experience and the need for mental health services, not all government agencies or insurance companies recognize it. This makes it very difficult to obtain funding for preventative measures such as improving mental, emotional, and physical wellness. That seems pretty simple, but without the proper "data," it doesn't get funded. The ACE Study provides that data. Maybe it's not common sense to everyone, but to those of us who have lived the trauma, it tends to make sense that living in survival mode prevents you from being able to focus on meeting your basic needs of mental, emotional and physical wellness. It also impairs decision making ability and causes a wealth of undesired behaviors. This process started for me between the ages of seven and nine.

At that age, my parents went through a rough separation, leading to divorce. The house was filled with the classic screaming, fighting and occasional physical altercation, which led to my father's domestic violence charges and jail time in King County, near Seattle, Washington. My sister is six years older than me, and as a teenager, she coped with the stress in our home through drug use and seeking the wrong kind of attention in the streets. I had always viewed my mother as a source of strength, but quickly started to sense doubt and worry in the way she looked at me and the tone of her voice. It was different; it was scary. I remember the electricity being cut off at one point. To make the best of it, we used the top of our pellet burning fireplace to cook corn dogs. I pretended that we were picnicking as we sat on the living room floor to eat. I never put it together until writing this paragraph, but it has dawned on me that as an adult I have always kept a package of State Fair Corn Dogs in my freezer. It's funny how that works. It was just the two of us, as there was a restraining order on my father, while my sister had been sent away to a drug treatment facility.

Those bonding moments quickly turned to stress. My mother and I started arguing, much like siblings do. I became very domineering with my friends in an attempt to have some control over my life and emotions. The once tidy house became a disaster torn apart from top to bottom with a garage that began to mimic a Hoarder's episode. Inevitably, I lost my friends, and things continued to spiral out of control very quickly between my mother and me. The last memory I have of the two of us before the social worker picked me up for placement was chasing after her, using my BB gun to pry her bedroom door open. I had no idea what to do with the emotional pain I felt, and I no longer knew who I was.

I was told that my mother was sick and had to go to the hospital in Seattle when the Department of Human Services took me to a strange home. The first home was filled with a handful of foster children. *It was scary. The smells were odd. The people were odd. Nobody showed any affection*, and I slept on a pad in a room with two other boys. The neighbor kids were nice, so I spent every day out in the neighborhood or watching The Terminator in one of their homes. I'm pretty sure we watched it half a dozen times. Prior to my parents' divorce, I had attended a private Christian school and was not allowed to watch scary things or listen to secular radio stations. Watching movies and listening to music was a new-found excitement, but it also felt very bad not being in my home with my family. I would have preferred that to scary movies, and the 1990's hip-hop music of TLC and Kris Kross any day.

A couple of weeks after being placed in my first foster home, I remember seeing my mother's white car drive into the cul-de-sac. I was so excited to see her that I ran into the woods next to the house and jumped out to surprise her! As I approached with my arms open to hug her, my smile quickly faded. Instead of bending down to hold me, she spoke very firmly and said, "You're doing it too, aren't you! What were you doing out there? You're doing drugs just like your sister!" She quickly got back into her car, ignoring the foster mother who was attempting to get her to stop and talk. I went to the sleeping pad in the room and cried, staring at the strange walls and smelling the strange smells, wondering why I was there and having no control over my life or emotions. With my knowledge today, I have identified that this must have been a "respite" home, which takes children who need emergency placement, but does not hold them longer than 30 days. After a while, I was taken to a new home.

The woman in my new home was an older lady that said she was a friend of my mother's. I didn't believe her, but after having a conversation with my mother 20 years later, it turns out that she really was. Regardless, I felt safe with her. Her home was clean, had no strange odors, and there was a nice backyard to play in. I didn't do much other than sit, though. She gave me a stuffed koala bear that I still have in my basement today. I slept with it every night until more strangers came to pick me up. You never know how big of an impact one simple gesture may have. To me, that koala bear was huge. The new people said they were my aunt, uncle, grandma and grandpa from Iowa. My mother was never close to her family, which I later found out was related to her own emotional trauma from her childhood. This is probably why I wasn't aware that I had any extended relatives.

My newfound family members packed up all of our belongings and I waved goodbye to our old house, the only home I had ever known. My uncle drove the belongings to Iowa while I boarded the plane with my aunt. My sister remained in drug treatment and I later found out that my mother was in the mental health unit in Seattle. All of our family's belongings were placed in storage. My behaviors continued to worsen. I was constantly angry and did not know why. I fought my aunt on everything, even when it came to putting a coat on in the middle of a blizzard.

Within a couple of months, my mother and sister finally arrived in Iowa. For a split second I thought we were going to be a normal family again. My grandpa helped us get a trailer to live in and I started school. Reality quickly sunk in when I was lying in bed with the rain hitting the trailer's tin roof one night. I just felt like I wasn't the same kid anymore. I didn't have friends and felt isolated. My clothes were often unwashed and smelled of cat urine. One of my few fond memories from this time, though, was when my mother and I would often sit on her bed watching her 13 inch black and white television at night. Dave Letterman and I became pretty close, but those moments were just small mental breaks from reality. I didn't have change to buy snacks in the a-la-cart line at school, and by the time I was in seventh grade, I was barely passing my classes. I remember a teacher warning me that I was close to having to be held back a grade. That was the least of my worries.

My sister dropped out of school and had started to run with drug dealers. It was my understanding that she was also dealing a significant amount herself. My mother stopped having the same look of endearment. She was gone a lot and there were strange men in the trailer at all hours. One of them even threw a beer can at me when I told him to leave my mom alone and that

I wanted to see her. Apparently I was interrupting something in the bedroom. It took me a long time to figure out what I had interrupted.

I stopped sleeping very well. I also stopped going to school on a regular basis. I missed the bus and frequently had what are called psychosomatic symptoms, when my emotional pain literally caused physical ailments. I had headaches and stomach pains that seemed to improve when I complained to the nurse to get out of school in order for my aunt to pick me up and take me to her house for the rest of the day; a safe place.

When I was at home, I was frequently unsupervised, and lacked the guidance to develop a moral compass. I stole from cars and homes and created elaborate "school fundraising" schemes to go door-to-door in nearby towns and steal money. When my mother was home, we often fought. I remember a major physical altercation that led to me running out of the house to get away. When I returned home, a police officer was there warning me about being "locked up" for assault. I was only 11 years old. He never once asked me what happened.

Around this time, I spent a month in an inpatient pediatric mental health unit for "testing." They told me I was completely normal, but as soon as I went back to my home environment, my old behaviors came back. The next time something bad happened, a social worker picked me up and took me to a youth shelter for a few weeks. It happened again, and I began to wonder if I was going to be just like my sister and do drugs, because this next time I went to a shelter, I was at the same shelter that I remembered visiting her in. It was also the same shelter that I had my first sexual experience in. I didn't know what was happening, but an older teenage girl started touching me and teaching me how to kiss after I mistook a round foil-wrapped condom for a chocolate candy. I was waiting in the room while my mom and sister had a meeting with the shelter staff. When my sister wasn't in a facility, she wasn't around much, but I missed her like crazy.

After a couple of years had passed, I was able to see my father again. My dad flew me back to Seattle one summer where my magically childish mind had envisioned life being the same as before. On arrival, I found out the he had gotten married to a woman who had three of her own children. Instead of going to his house where I would recognize all of the smells and see similar household items, we went straight to his new wife's house. She was of Asian decent, and there were a bunch of strange new smells that I had never smelled before. It was nighttime when I arrived by plane, and I went straight to bed in a bunk bed where another boy was sleeping. After maybe 10 minutes, I went out to the living room, and stood still in one spot as tears poured forth from my eyes. My dad took me back to his place and I slept in his bed all the way through the night for the first time in a long time. I went back to visit every summer from then on.

One summer, my sister gave me some cash for my trip to see Dad. Another summer, she bought me a brand new pair of Nike shoes from the expensive store in the mall. I was accustomed to the twenty-five or fifty cent racks at the local Salvation Army, so getting these shoes was the highlight of my entire year! I wore them until there were holes in the soles, and thought of my cool sister every time I put them on. I wanted to do everything she did. The things that stuck out in my head of my memories with her were riding in a car with a really loud bass system and having cool shoes. To this day, I still follow the instructions she gave me to be careful and not bend the heel of the shoe when putting them on so that I don't ruin the nice shape. I never let go of those memories, and even still listen to the same music that I heard in her car. If you ever come on a ride with me in my car, you will likely experience my subwoofers bumping the same loud bass and 2pac rap songs as back then. It isn't an everyday occurrence anymore, but I treat it like soul food. Every once in a while, you just need a memory that feels nostalgic, especially when there are so many memories that you wish you didn't have. Both the good and bad things stick with you forever. I found this out the hard way.

By the time I was in eighth grade, my home life was worsening. Some things happened that I still to this day don't feel comfortable sharing. My aunt allowed me to stay with her and gave me the option of living with her and my uncle permanently or moving back to Seattle with my Dad. I couldn't't fathom living with a family that wasn't mine and not being able to have my Dad be just "my Dad," so I opted to stay with my aunt and uncle. A stable home life allowed me to focus on just being a kid and student. I went from almost failing in school to being recognized as the most improved in the class, at the end of the year. Receiving that recognition became one of my favorite feel-good memories. It wasn't something that was voted on, but it was two teachers who talked together to choose someone to recognize for this award. They might have done the same for 10 other kids they saw struggling, but in that moment, it made me feel pretty special.

I started to be able to make friends, but I always got weird looks when they found out that I didn't live with my Mom and Dad. This made me feel very awkward; much like it does for many young people who don't have, what most would consider, a "normal" home. When you feel awkward, this fear of rejection makes it very difficult to let someone in so I always kept people at a distance. I got involved with sports and started playing baseball, however my passion quickly became the one-on-one combat of wrestling. There was just something about knowing the win was all up to me. At first I got my butt whooped, but soon I felt myself getting stronger and swifter with my moves. This realization slowly helped me believe in myself more than I had in a long time. When you no longer receive your identity, confidence, and sense of self from your parents, you tend to find ways to fill the void. Wrestling was the first void-filler that helped me stay out of trouble. With something productive to focus on, I no longer ran the streets, stole, or even smoked cigarettes. Smoking was an unfortunate "cool" habit that I picked up around the age of 11 or 12, as I was stealing cartons from gas stations to sell them by the pack to older kids.

As I became a teen, I made it a priority to visit my mother almost every Sunday, even if the 12 to 15 psych drugs she took daily prevented her from being coherent enough to talk or remember that I was there. No matter what I went through, she was still my Mom and no matter who helped me or took care of me, that is how it always stayed. There is definitely something to be said for a child's loyalty.

CHAPTER 3

LOYALTY RUNS DEEP

"Just as my aunt evicted me from her house, stepping back and refusing to rescue someone could help them to realize..."

Not only is there a lot to be said for a child's loyalty, but familial loyalty in general is one of the strongest ties we have. It makes sense; taking care of your family or tribe/inner circle hearkens back to hunter-gatherer days. Families that stayed together stayed alive. Now, those blood ties still exist, but there are some circumstances, such as when there is addiction, abuse, or mental health issues where family ties can end up causing emotional trauma, stress, and financial problems. Let's say your parents are always borrowing money, never paying the money back, and need to be constantly bailed out (either figuratively or literally from jail) like an irresponsible teen. Or like me, you have a sister who struggled with addiction? How are we to be there for our family members without sacrificing our own health and well-being? It is very easy to fall into the trap of feeling guilty if you can't always be there for them, as this feeling is so ingrained that you are supposed to love, support, and protect your family at all costs. However, love and support can appear in many disguises. Here are some tips to help your family members in need:

Know When to Say No

It may seem somewhat funny in a section about supporting family that the first part is about not doing something, but trust me, being able to identify when to be assertive and step back from the situation will benefit you, and quite likely benefit your family members, as well. You may have heard it said at some point in your life, "You have to help them, they're your father (or mother)", or "You need to stick up for your family members, no matter what". Although obviously you owe a lot to your family, especially your parents as they're the sole reason you're alive and with us today, you have to realize that as adults, they need to be accountable for their own actions as well.

What if your sister is in a fight with her boyfriend? You step in to intervene, only to find out that the reason they are fighting is because she cheated on him and moved out suddenly, while still owing him two months worth of rent. This seems like a scenario where it is absolutely understandable that her boyfriend would be angry. In this type of circumstance, you should probably allow your sister her own journey. If she's upset afterwards, let her vent, maybe ask her some questions about why she made the decisions she did. There comes a point, though, where you need to back up and think, "Yeah, they screwed up, but this is not my problem." If you continually swoop in and save the day, you allow their pattern of irresponsibility to continue. When referring to addiction, this action is called enabling. Enabling allows the addict to continue their negative lifestyle without consequences to their behavior e.g. giving them a place to stay, giving them money, maybe even allowing them to have drugs. This may be some hard truth to swallow, especially if you are inadvertently enabling a loved one right now, but you have to know enabling helps no one. It continues patterns of bad behavior, increases the risk of health problems the longer they use the drug, and causes you distress.

Of course you want your mother, father, uncle, and others in your life, to be happy and healthy, but you need to also think about you. Is it really worth it to sacrifice things that keep you stable for someone that is going to keep coming back needing the same help? Why should you keep lending your cousin money for "rent" when you know he's going to spend it on cocaine? You're not doing yourself or your family any favors if you expend yourself to the point of exhaustion. Sometimes detaching yourself from the situation can be the greatest gift you can give to a family member. *Just as my aunt evicted me from her house, stepping back and refusing to rescue others could help them to realize* that how they've been living their life is hurting themselves and others. I later did the same by not talking to my sister for nearly two years once I learned her drug use was impacting my nephew. This allowed us to learn and grow at our own pace. After connecting, it took several years of slowly rekindling our relationship to find a new appreciation for each other as adults. I would even venture to say that we have developed a close relationship. Even if your family member isn't doing drugs or abusing alcohol, don't enable other traits that cause distress e.g. they constantly try to stir up drama and guilt you into contributing. Strategically detach yourself and know that tough love can be extremely helpful.

Fairy-Tale Endings

As I mentioned previously, tough love can help someone break out of a funk. But there isn't a catch-all strategy for every situation, and sometimes tough love does not help shake your loved ones out of their high-risk behavior. Maybe they keep up their same patterns and go into debt, lose their job, alienate themselves from their friends. Maybe they go to rehab, but it doesn't work and they fall back into old habits. You have to prepare yourself for the possibility that you may not be able to fix them. You have to be okay with that. Not everyone gets a fairy-tale ending where the bad guy falls into a pit of lava and you rescue the princess. Sadly, some people go their whole lives without changing their ways, and have a miserable time because of it. As my reference to the Adverse Childhood Experience (ACE) study suggests, such patterns often even lead to early death.

This thought can be depressing, especially if you are a person who prides yourself on accomplishing goals, problem solving, and being a loving and caring friend or family member. But you are not an all-powerful deity, and there are some things you don't have any control over. The family member you want to help, for example your father, is an adult. As an adult, he is an autonomous individual who is free to make his own decisions. Because he is someone capable of making his own decisions, this also entails that he is accountable for his decisions. If he continues to make choices that help him lose friends and alienate people, there isn't much you can do apart from offer advice ("Why, maybe next time don't get drunk and cuss out your sister at the family reunion"). If he chooses not to listen to your advice, then you've done all you can do. To a certain extent, the same goes for children and adolescents in your life. Of course, in that case you would enforce rules and implement punishment along with the advice.

It may be extremely frustrating realizing that ultimately you can't control a person's every action, especially when their actions seem to be bad ones! Whenever you start to feel upset that what you're saying to or doing for your family member isn't working, say to yourself, "They are an adult. I have to allow them their own journey." This can help reduce the inclination to beat yourself up thinking, "I could have done more!" Sometimes, you give it your best, and that's all you can do.

Knowing When and How to Say Yes

Yes, there are ways you can help your family, friends, and overbearing clients or co-workers! Knowing when to say yes is intuitive; you know your family members best, so you should be able to reasonably guess when they're running in the same negative circles and when they actually want to turn their life around. When it comes to a friend or co-worker that you are not extremely close with, you may want to be more skeptical as it may be more difficult to identify their true intent than with someone you are close with and can read more easily.

Regardless, being there for them can make all the difference in their world. That $5000 loan you give to Uncle Jim to start up his landscaping business may be exactly what he needed to get back on his feet and into stable employment. If you're wary about trusting that person, especially if they have lied to you in the past, take some time to see if they're genuine. Trust takes time, and rebuilding trust takes even longer, so take that time for yourself to observe their actions and see if they actually want to make different choices. Don't let yourself get pressured into making a quick decision if you are unsure.

There are different ways to say yes or be helpful. As an adjunct professor, I still occasionally teach third and fourth year undergraduate nursing students the basics of caring for pediatric patients in the hospital setting. I find the most beneficial way to help my students learn and grow is to set up the foundation and teach them the skills to find the right answers, rather than telling them the answers outright. You know, that old saying, "Give a man a fish and he eats for a day. Teach a man to fish and he eats for a lifetime" (cliché saying but it's true!). When you provide support to your friend or loved one, don't try to do everything for them, but instead allow them the means to achieve success for themselves. Apart from giving that person a sense of empowerment, providing frameworks rather than all the answers avoids the risk that person will feel you are trying to control or "baby" them.

What does this help look like? Let's say your brother has Bipolar Type I Disorder. He has been treated with lithium from time to time, but sometimes forgets to take it, or goes off the medication because he thinks he can handle his moods himself. When he enters into mania, he goes on extravagant spending sprees, ends up snapping at loved ones, and gets into fights at bars. During his cycle into depression, he has suicidal thoughts and self-medicates with alcohol and various street drugs. He was hospitalized after his most recent mania, and when he comes back home, he claims that he wants to make a commitment to keeping a stable mood and promises he will stay on lithium. He has made these promises before and has broken them time and again. But this time seems different and you believe him when he says he is going to stay on medication and will support him however you can. Rather than constantly checking on him or searching his pill bottles to see if he's taking the correct dosage, maybe set up a plan with your brother that you will check in every few days to make sure he's stable, or give him a pill organizer so he won't skip a day through forgetfulness.

This is merely one example, and I am not making a comment either way on whether to take medication for psychiatric illness or not. Instead, this is meant to illustrate that you can help someone without completely taking away their independence. Communicate your expectations with your loved one; set up an arrangement that you will feel comfortable with, and you think will help them, without it being too overbearing for you.

CHAPTER 4

A ROUGH TRANSITION

"To no surprise, there are very serious suicide rates that parallel this time of distress."

M y nephew was born just before I started high school and I did everything in my power to make sure he had what he needed. I used my allowance to buy him clothes and cool gifts, and used my newly established woodworking skills to refinish a crib that I bought at the local Salvation Army. Being in a stable home helped me see what it was like to live a middle-class life and have everything I needed. I wanted him to experience this as well, and have nice things. I did my best, but quickly realized the true cost when "things" weren't stolen. Around this same time, I still had 100 community service hours to work off from getting busted for theft, so I spent time cleaning a church. I was given responsibility and was trusted to do a good job. I worked hard and started to find pride and value in a sense of accomplishment.

As soon as I was old enough to work, I constantly looked for ways to make money. Mowing lawns and getting paid to help my aunt and uncle do projects no longer did the trick. I had a taste of what "normal" felt like and I never wanted to have to depend on anyone again. I made up my mind that I would always be able to buy what I wanted, have a cool car with subwoofer bass in the trunk, and never let anyone tell me I can't do something that I know is possible. I decided that if there was no way to do something, I would find a way and support it myself. I held a steady job from that point on. This dedication followed me through my high school years, but temporarily disappeared for an extended time during my senior year and the following summer. In foster care, this time period usually lands around the age of 18 and is referred to as "transitioning out of the system," or "aging out." Every young person goes through this struggle of leaving high school and "finding what to be in life," but for a young adult who lacks a strong sense of self and healthy supportive relationships, this is the time period when most simply give up. *To no surprise, there are very serious suicide rates that parallel this time of distress.*

I started having nightmares. Several times I woke up in cold sweats, holding back tears and experiencing flashbacks from events that occurred when I was younger. One time a dream brought back suppressed memories of when our family first split apart. I jumped up in tears yelling "Daddy!" There was a time when I never thought I would see my father again. This memory came back when I was 18, just as I was beginning to question the purpose of my life. My mind had blocked these memories for many years, but for some reason, my guard was down and they crept back as fast as they had been forgotten. I felt like I was living between two worlds and started to give up. I started to wonder who I was and thought that I wasn't good enough to do any better. I felt bad that I was doing well while my family was not. As I was still loyal to them, this was a difficult struggle for me. During this time period, I was told once that I was probably more likely to be dead or in jail before I turned 18 than to actually graduate from high school. I was so extrinsically influenced that I started to believe this and reverted back to my old behaviors.

Critical Thinking Moment: Generational cycles of a lack of education paired with abuse can leave a legacy of hell, but you have the power to break them or be the change-agent for someone else. Do you have what it takes? Are you willing and emotionally stable enough to be there for someone else when they really need you? Sometimes simply giving it your best is exactly what is needed even when you don't feel ready. There is never a perfect time to start.

Reverting to negative behaviors made transitioning to adulthood for myself interesting, to say the least. There is not enough space in this book to explain the many situations I allowed myself to get into that I now find shocking. I stole, broke into homes, drank, and partied. Seeking sex as a way to fill the many emotional voids became a pattern that impeded my ability to develop meaningful emotional bonds for most of my life. I treated my aunt worse than ever and after she couldn't take it anymore she kicked me out; no doubt about it, it was tough love. The eviction came with tears in her eyes and I'm sure it was extremely difficult to do, but it was the best thing for me and I knew it immediately. I wasn't mad and I didn't argue. I just drove down the gravel road away from their home in silence, with tears running down my cheeks, knowing it was yet another result of my inability to express myself and communicate effectively. I was a know-it-all; not because I knew anything, but because I knew I didn't know enough and I hated the fact that I knew there was more to life, but couldn't find what it was. One way or another, I had to seem like I knew who I was and hold my ground, even when I was wrong, even at the cost of a home and food. I was homeless for a few weeks, sneaking in and out of my girlfriend's house to sleep until

I managed to get a second job and an apartment.

The lifestyle that I had at this point was a perfect example of an important topic that will be discussed later: Survival Mode. I thought that I thrived in chaos, but what I truly craved was stability. Without strong ties to a family, I naturally started to seek stability elsewhere. I have met some young people who seek stability through spending every day after school at a friend's house who's family cooks dinner every day. Some adult friends of mine have sought stability in their otherwise unstable and unfulfilling lives by joining a church or becoming a consistent volunteer for a cause they believe in. Personally, I highly discourage finding your identity in your work as some people do. Yet, during my rough transition to adulthood, my own work became the one stable thing that I could always count on. In high school, it was my job as a residential counselor caring for mentally and physically handicapped adults. In college, it became working in a nursing home as a Certified Nursing Assistant (CNA) and later as a psychiatric technician. When nothing in life seemed normal, going to work the same day and time each week felt like home. My employers provided me with health insurance, consistency, and even sometimes meals. They also provided me with the education of many life lessons that still serve me to this day.

In the Critical Thinking Moment, I said that there is no "right" time to be a change-agent or support for someone who has experienced trauma or is in a generational cycle. One of the first steps is to allow the person to tell their story. Through regularly providing advice I have found, through trial and error, that it is the absolute most important step. For those of you who may be seeking to overcome your own past, Chapter 10 will provide a specific tool for finding your voice.

When it comes to helping others, either in your professional life or merely as friends, you may have someone approach you that needs to speak with you about some tough topics, such as sexual assault, abuse, addiction, or criminal activities. This experience can be daunting and many people balk at traumatized individuals opening up to them, worried they aren't "qualified" or "won't know the right thing to say" or potentially even judging the person negatively. You don't need to be a psychologist to help someone in need (although that can definitely give you a greater level of understanding), but I do have some insight from my time as a mental health crisis worker. These are tips that I have learned from others and successfully implemented through having spent several years talking with mentally ill, depressed, psychotic or suicidal individuals every week. Here's what you should keep in mind if someone opens up to you about their trauma:

The Importance of Voicing

You don't need to be a trauma theorist to know that speaking about your problems is therapeutic. After a frustrating, busy day at work, venting to a friend about what irritated you can make you feel immediately better. When you have experienced a traumatic event or events, being able to share with a caring, receptive person is essential to the healing process, allowing you to start to understand the trauma and work through your suffering. A traumatic experience can leave a blind spot in the narrative of your life, through your mind trying to suppress the pain. Part of the reason people experience traumatic flashbacks is because their mind does not understand; it is trying to make sense of why or how this could have happened. Psychoanalyst Dori Laub writes that, "the emergence of the [trauma] narrative which is being listened to—and heard—is...the process and the place wherein the cognizance, the "knowing" of the event is given birth to" (57). Listening to someone tell their story is one of the first steps for them to overcome emotional trauma. If a friend comes to you needing to confide, make time for them, I can't stress how important this is for their psychological well-being. If you know that someone is wounded, offer to let them tell their story (if you feel comfortable). Knowing that there is someone there who is willing to bear witness to their hurt can open the door to healing.

For those of you who are anxious to share your hurt and pain, be wise in who you choose to expose your traumatic experiences to. The very exposure that you seek to enable healing may be what some people use to judge you which can potentially re-traumatize a healing wound. Seeking close friends who can keep you focused, even when you are upset, is ideal.

Active Listening and Silence

When a person tells you their story, what they need is to be heard, really heard by the person they are talking to. If a survivor feels that their words fall on deaf ears, it may cause fresh pain. Show through your body language that you are engaged in what they are saying, make eye contact, or nod your head. You may also want to say little things like, "mhm", "okay", or "what happened next?" Don't let your mind wander thinking about what to say once they finish talking, be in the moment, take in each phrase, each breath, each tear. Only once they have finished should you then start thinking about how you want to respond.

There will probably be times during the narrative where the survivor will fall silent. Trauma is confusing, it bewilders, disrupts, and injures. It is understandable that sometimes they won't know what to say, or will be so overcome with the emotional affect of re-envisioning what happened to them that it will be painful to continue. Saying the words, "I was raped," or "I'm addicted to crack", may be very frightening to say because in saying those words, it may finally make it "real" for the person after a lifetime of avoiding a painful reality. If the storyteller falls silent, be patient with their pause. Don't try to urge them on, but allow them the space of that silence. Take their hand, offer them a tissue if they need it, or stay still. This type of safe therapeutic touch is often taught in nursing colleges and can make all the difference in the world. If, and only if it seems appropriate, ask them if they'd like to continue or what happened next. Most importantly, do not interject unsolicited advice or tell them your own stories. Let them own the moment and be heard. Sometimes that is all it takes for the healing process to begin.

Speak Wisely

Carefully consider your words after the survivor has finished telling their story. It is completely acceptable if you have nothing to say, or if all you can respond with is, "that sucks." A simple statement acknowledging their pain is sometimes all they want; it might help them feel less alone. Bad experiences often create a very lonely place in our minds.

Just like venting after a bad day of work, when someone tells you their story, sometimes all they need is a butt in the seat, a caring person to speak at without fear of being judged. In the panic of trying to find things to say, some people blurt out clichés. Please try to avoid something that may come across as corny or victim-blaming, such as, "Are you sure it wasn't something you did?" Another thing that might seem strange to avoid saying is "I'm sorry." What is someone's default response when they hear "I'm sorry"? They say, "It's okay." It's not really helpful. Instead let them know that what happened to them is terrible and no one deserves to experience what they experienced. If there is more to the story that needs to be discussed, that can wait until their mind has had a chance to "vomit" their story and allow their emotions to calm. This will allow a much more logical response as opposed to the emotional fight that you might face during their moment of crisis.

Communicate to the storyteller that you are glad that they trusted you enough to share their story. Thank them for sharing. Tell them you love and care about them. In any way you can, let them know that they have been brave and made a good choice confiding in you.

Follow-Up

So you have helped someone begin some essential steps towards trauma recovery, they felt acknowledged and loved. Ongoing support is essential in helping them work through their trauma. In a couple days, make sure you follow up with them. There is nothing complex about the follow up, even asking them how they're doing and chatting for a few minutes will reinforce that you are someone who cares and that they can trust. If you feel it is appropriate, you can speak to them about the story they shared, but even if you talk to them about something mundane, like if they liked the new movie they saw the other day, it can make a big difference. It isn't so much about what words you say, but that there is someone there that cares.

For close friends and family members, this is very difficult, especially if the situation may have impacted you negatively. In a workplace, it can create a very awkward vibe. However, avoiding the topic because it made you feel uncomfortable or have your own vendetta does nothing more than precipitate more hurt and pain for everyone involved. It is at your discretion whether you feel the person will be receptive to a direct conversation about the prior issue or simple small talk. Even in professional settings, people need to know that someone cares.

CHAPTER 5

A DEFINING MOMENT
A Life Lesson on Selflessness

*"He struggled like I did, but in
a different way."*

After a lifetime of experiences that I perceived as traumatic, I found it very difficult to express emotions as a teen. The most difficult were those of extreme happiness or sadness. If I wasn't over-reacting, which I was known to do occasionally, I generally stayed in a constant state of non-reaction. Many people who life in extreme states of unhappiness and internal pain resort to "cutting." They cut themselves not as a suicide attempt, but often as a way to "feel something" so they "know" they are alive because "everything inside feels dead." Those are specific quotes several of my previous clients have used. In my line of work, I have most often seen this behavior in individuals diagnosed as bipolar or borderline personality disorder, but it can show in any person struggling with severe traumatic experiences. I was never one to "cut", but I am willing to bet that the numbness I felt at that time was very similar to that of the people who cut "to feel something."

Fortunately, I had a light-bulb moment in my teen working years that helped me "feel" again. That moment has proven to be a lesson that continues to serve me throughout my adult years. It occurred while working as a Residential Counselor, taking care of mentally handicapped adults at the age of 17. The lesson learned was that of selflessness.

Historically, I was of the mindset that "you do what you have to do to get by," so this lesson was a bit of an unexpected shock to me. This mindset of "watching out for number one" was prevalent even in my teen years and showed in my initial motivation to work in health care. The sole reason I applied for the job was because I heard that I could make more than seven dollars per hour. I did not know what the job was, nor did I care. I was 16 when I applied, and focused on the fact that seven dollars and twenty-six cents per hour was two dollars and eleven cents more than the minimum wage of $5.15 in the year 2000. I felt that this higher rate of pay would allow me to more easily avoid the shame that came along with not having money to go out to eat with others or buy what I wanted, when I wanted. To a certain extent I was right, but the experience I gained was more valuable that I could have imagined.

Recognizing how amazing it felt to see a physically incapacitated and mentally delayed 21 year old in a wheel chair jump for joy (as much as he could) when I simply took the time to talk "guy talk" was an eye-opener for me. Strangely, that lit a fire in my soul. *He struggled like I did, but in a different way.* He sought acceptance the same as I did, but with an open heart and mind; one that did not hold walls up or react to potential attachments. It made me want to be there for him, not just as a job, but also as a friend. At that time, I not only experienced what it was like to be selfless, but also how much it burned inside of me that I wanted to fight for the underdog.

While spending my evenings wiping stool from incontinent residents and taking them for walks, I would play out in my mind what I would say or do if someone disrespected that 21 year old wheel chair-ridden kind soul that rolled next to me in our small town streets. Sometimes I thought about what I would say and how many threatening curse words I would use. Other times, I thought about using my wrestling moves to defend and protect. My frontal lobe was so far from maturity that there wasn't much I wouldn't consider; all were viable options. Helping someone else feel safe and secure became more important to me than my own safety. That was an interesting feeling and it felt good to know that I had the control and responsibility to give someone something that I always wanted; safety, security, and unconditional acceptance. I hadn't felt that way since before my parents first separated.

Critical Thinking Moment: When was the last time you stood up for the underdog? It doesn't have to be someone who is being verbally or physically attacked, sometimes it can just be doing something nice. When was the last time you did something nice without expecting something in return? Giving of your time, energy and emotions to others is one of the most fulfilling things in the world. Medical research has shown that giving your time to help others improves your mood by releasing "feel good" chemicals in your body called endorphins.

Unfortunately, this life lesson and burning desire to fight for the underdog would eventually turn to a dimly lit flame and lie dormant for several years. Continued negative family dynamics and a string of unhealthy relationships through my young adult years caused me to often forget about these lessons and resort to selfishness. Life quickly became all about me, myself, and I.

Viewed from the outside, many others often saw this "looking out for number one" attitude as a personality disorder. In the sense of the dictionary definition of a "diagnosis" I suppose they were right. But for me, it was again simply survival mode. I lived in a constant state of insecurity, anxiousness, and fear of persecution. Although such a list of "symptoms" quickly earns one a diagnosis, and often a prescription, there were reasons for my symptoms. Unfortunately, not one therapist or physician asked about why I felt the way I did. When I was 19, a trip to my family doctor for difficulty sleeping due to worry and fear of persecution resulted in a script for a sleep aid and an antidepressant. Apparently I displayed symptoms of personality disorders and potential psychosis.

In actuality, I was balancing my emotionally traumatic history with a lifestyle that consistently compounded my trauma and perpetuated generational cycles. The fear of persecution was simply due to the fact that I had broken the law several times and was constantly worried that the knock on the door or the unidentified number calling my phone would be a detective. It would not have been the first time. Believe me, this makes it really difficult to sleep. Since I was always trying to figure out how the legal system worked and if there might be loopholes, I was willing to ask questions even to a doctor just to seek some insight that might ease my mind.

I was far too stubborn to put two and two together and realize that if I simply quit the illegal or otherwise negative behaviors, I would not have to worry. I can attest to the fact that when you are living a messy life, it is very difficult to see your own mess. And honestly, even when you do see it, you are so accustomed to it that doing what it takes to change seems impossible. I wasn't ready to change, but the lesson of selflessness shined through again while I was still 19.

I had moved away to study business, but continued to be plagued with worry about my mother, sister, and nephew. My nephew had been bounced from home to home, staying with my mother, his father, and his paternal grandmother, depending on which one was most stable at the time. I had observed drugs being abused and sold around my nephew, and I wanted to do anything I could to help. I had many thoughts of hunting down each person who ever wronged my nephew. I even got in my car, pumped the bass in the trunk, drove 90 minutes back home, and cruised around looking to have a "talk" with some of the people involved in anything that had the potential to cause emotional damage to my nephew. Luckily, I never found them, so I had to find a new approach. Being a student with a part time job didn't allow me to do much, but that summer I made an economic decision to stand up for the underdog. I decided that I would take custody of my nephew as soon as I could afford to.

Many of the business students who had graduated the previous year talked about how they struggled to find jobs that paid more than $30,000, and the jobs they did get required working excessive hours. It didn't seem like they had fun lives, and I knew that I needed to make more than 30 thousand to be able to take care of my nephew. Once again, I made the economic decision to capitalize on health care. One of the nurses I worked with had previously told me it was easy to make 40 to 50K working three 12 hour shifts per week as a registered nurse. So, I did what had to be done; not for myself, but for the underdog, my nephew. Seven days before the next semester began, I took my resume and transcripts to the nearby private nursing college and enrolled to become a registered nurse.

It's awesome how things come full circle when you allow yourself to be used for the greater good. My aunt and uncle had taken me in and given me the opportunity to have a stable life that taught me the basic principles of hard work, dedication, morals, and good judgment. At the age of 19, I made the decision that I was going to do the same for my nephew; however, it wasn't an easy decision. It seems that when I have big decisions to make, the answers always come to me in my dreams. It has never been a pleasant experience because every time I dream about a decision

I need to make, it always turns into a nightmare. I dreamt that I was never going to see my nephew again because the Department of Human Services, the state child welfare entity responsible for keeping kids safe, took him just as they had once taken me. Even in my dream, I knew it seemed like the right thing to do, but I couldn't bear having a stranger do it. I woke up in tears at 4AM, knowing that I had to step up. There was still a long road ahead of me, but I was willing to tread the waters to the end of the earth to make sure that my nephew never left our family.

I bought my white and blue scrubs, a blood pressure cuff, and stethoscope and off to nursing school I went.

CHAPTER 6

STARING IN THE MIRROR

"This made me feel a little better about 'getting stuck in the psych unit'"

I had been working in a nursing home as a CNA (Certified Nursing Assistant), so the transition to nursing school was not a major shock. However, I did feel that I needed to obtain hospital experience in order to be considered for higher paying and more skillful jobs. This again would allow me to better fulfill my desire to buy what I wanted, when I wanted, and depend on nobody else but myself. Quite the opposite of Salvation Army shoes and empty cupboards. I applied to the hospital that was associated with my new school. Every other time I had applied for jobs, I had heard back within a week or two, and if I didn't, I would put a suit on and walk into their office to shake their hand. But the big hospital was intimidating to me, and there were so many offices it was hard to know who to talk to. When I finally had the courage to ask someone in the Human Resources Department, they informed me that they did not allow applicants to speak with managers. I was so accustomed to finding ways to make things happen that I was very discouraged when the HR lady shot me down. Three months later, I finally got a call.

I had applied to a surgical floor and an intensive care unit, so I found it very strange that the call I received came from the manager of the mental health unit. The units I applied for must not have felt that I had adequate medical experience. I assumed they passed my resume to the psych ward where I was sure nobody would actually want to work. I was extremely hesitant, but I had heard that if you are hired at a large facility, then you are allowed to transfer after six months and you have a better chance of getting the job you want as an internal applicant. So, I continued to do what I needed to do and became a mental health technician. The unit manager later informed me that they often request people who have a background in long-term care due to the amount of patience that one often develops through caring for those who are unable to care for themselves. This made me feel a little better about "getting stuck in the psych unit" when I had applied elsewhere. Honestly, it felt pretty good to know that I had been requested. Knowing that it was a positive request that brought me to work in the psych unit made me feel kind of silly for having assumed the worst. This became one of my favorite lessons that I've learned about assumptions.

The other lesson was during my 8th grade shop class when I used a drill bit that was meant for wood to attempt to drill through a piece of metal. When my teacher asked me, "What in the hell" I was doing, I responded with, "I assumed that since…" He cut me off and asked me if I knew what the first three letters of "assumption" spelled, continuing to berate me, informing that when I make assumptions, it makes an ass out of both him and me. It sounds rather harsh, but it is actually one of my favorite memories. The reference of the first three letters in the word assumption is also some good material that has definitely been re-used.

Critical Thinking Moment: Have you ever made

> assumptions about people or situations that you just don't understand? It is very easy to judge, but it takes more patience and kindness to understand. That is why there is such negative stigma surrounding those who suffer from mental and emotional issues, especially in America. There may be very valid traumatic reasons for someone's socially awkward behaviors, but we as society place judgment through assumptions. Is there someone in your life who you could be more accepting of?

I continued to learn the importance of not making assumptions during my first six months working as a psych tech. I met all types of interesting people, and every time I thought I had an idea about what someone was like or what they had been through, I was completely wrong. For the most part, my job consisted of very mundane tasks. The most important task was to do a head count every 15 minutes. This was to ensure that each person was accounted for and hadn't escaped. Some of them were court ordered due to crimes committed while behaving in a psychotic manner, for their own safety and prevention of self-harm, or for substance abuse treatment. I also had the responsibility during rounds to make sure that everyone was still breathing, and nobody was hurting themselves or others.

I became very sympathetic for many of our patients who seemed to be such good people, but just had really bad luck. Every once in a while, I would see a staff member react to a patient in a way that would make the situation worse. I remember one specific time a nurse was attempting to force a lower functioning 30 year old man to take his medicine a certain way, as he wasn't cooperating. He wouldn't take it from her, but he would take it from someone else. He wanted to hold the cup of pills instead of having someone else pour them in his mouth. That is how he was accustomed to taking his meds.

I'm pretty sure this specific nurse had many of her own unsolved emotional traumas that impaired her ability to see the big picture of what was happening. She became defensive at his request for someone else to give him his pills and demanded that he cooperate with her instruction because she was "in charge." She kept demanding his compliance to the point where he became very explosive. Because he was a lower functioning adult, his behaviors were similar to that of a 3 year old throwing a temper-tantrum. Yet, he was about 220 pounds, and stood at 6' 2." The nurse quickly ran into the locked nurse's station to secure her own safety and called a "Code Green." At this point, the unit had to be cleared, all patients had to return to their rooms, and half a dozen staff members, including a few security officers, would soon arrive in an attack mode ready to pounce on any patient that might be physically out of control. This is a standard response for violent threats in a hospital setting, but is often over-utilized when dealing with those in mental and emotional distress. I believe such over-utilization stems from a lack of awareness of how to incorporate empathy in crisis intervention. Regardless, It's a good thing I was a wrestler, because being the only physically capable staff member on the unit at the time meant that my inferred job was to begin the process of restraining anyone who became physically violent.

I really liked this guy, so it killed me to have to take him down. It wasn't an easy task considering I only weighed about 150 dripping wet. I had finished my senior wrestling season wrestling at the 140. We grappled for a few minutes until the troops arrived. The security guards weren't real cops, but sometimes they liked to act like they were. One of them started punching the patient's shoulder to force him to submit his arm for restraint. That same security guard actually threatened the obviously mentally delayed individual with jail time for physical assault. I was kind of glad that he got punched at that point considering no courtroom in the world would ever declare that specific patient as competent in his decision to throw a punch. Unfortunately, \ the patient also kicked me in the chest, so I took on the feat of holding his legs down. After several minutes had passed, seven of us carried him into the restraint room, one that was padded on all sides. There was one metal bed sitting in the center of the room where we tied him down in 4-point restraints. This is when each limb is extended onto the bed with a thick bracelet-like cloth restraint strapped to each wrist and ankle. This is a common practice in most mental health units and psychiatric hospitals, but there are currently many groups moving to create legislation that is much more restrictive on when such restrictive practices are utilized in clinical and residential settings.

We then pulled his pants down, and injected Haldol and Ativan into his thigh. These two drugs are known as a "special cocktail" that knocks out the individual; some call it a "chemical restraint." When we put someone in restraints, it was my job to sit with them. Sometimes I would talk to them, while other times I would sit in silence documenting my observations. I had to document that they were breathing, offer them opportunities to use the urinal or drink water, and check their pulse near the restraints to ensure they weren't too tight. Sometimes this part of the job also required me to be on the receiving end of endless verbal abuse and hatred. I usually couldn't blame them. Sometimes I still feel sorry for the patients in these situations who are unlucky enough to have someone watching over them who doesn't care enough to loosen the straps when they are too tight, or worse, tighten them out of spite in the heat of the moment.

I dimmed the lights to help with the calming process, but was struggling to remain calm myself. I wasn't angry with the patient for leaving a footprint on my chest; I was angry with the nurse whose lack of self-awareness resulted in a horrible outcome that, more likely than not, could have been easily avoided. After the patient had woken from his sleep, he was calm, polite, and apologetic. He had an ashamed look on his face when he apologized to me and pouted like a toddler who was just put in time out. I placed my hand on his shoulder and said, "It's not your fault; let's get ready for dinner and we can talk about it later." It wasn't until later in my career as a Mental Health Crisis Worker that I realized that this simple gesture of reassuring someone during, or after, a tough situation does wonders for your ability to connect with them and work towards improved outcomes in the future.

Before dinner, I decided it was time for me to call this nurse out. I felt like I had to fight for the underdog. I worked to remain calm, kind, and professional. Still, I had to bite my lip to keep from blurting out the curse words I had practiced in my head two years prior, while walking with my 21 year old wheel-chair ridden friend. I approached her as she was coolly documenting the issues that she created. "I really don't feel that how you handled that situation was appropriate," I said. "It seems like that entire situation could have been avoided. He didn't need to be tackled and sedated. Why didn't you just get someone else and let him hold the cup?"

"Well, I'm his nurse and that's my decision," she replied.

I complained to another nurse who I respected as a wise mother figure, and she agreed with me, but was not willing to do anything more than give me an understanding half-smile. I went home frustrated, replaying the wrestling match in my mind.

The next day, I showed up for work and marched right in to the director's office to explain the situation. I was breathing heavily and working hard to get him to agree with me. His face was blank; I wasn't sure if he understood my sense of urgency. I tried to embellish the story as much as possible. After I blurted out every detail he replied, "It sounds like that really bothers you." I couldn't understand how he was not upset! He then asked me what I thought should happen. I couldn't come up with a response; I just wanted the nurse to understand how she made the situation worse than it needed to be and to stop behaving that way. I had seen her behave inappropriately before, but never that badly.

Unfortunately, you can't force others to be self-aware, so the director simply said, "You know, you're probably right; it probably could have been handled differently and we might talk about better ways to handle those situations in the future. But you might want to consider how much this is bothering that nurse. She seems to be doing just fine, so you're only torturing yourself. Everyone else has moved on from this situation, but it obviously kept you up last night. I'm glad to know you are passionate about helping our patients, but at what cost to your own sanity?"

Apparently, I still had some trouble controlling my reactions, even in a professional setting. Considering there were no rules broken and no permanent damage done, I probably should have been content with voicing my opinion to the nurse. I wanted justice, and to see the nurse suffer through being proven wrong and admitting her wrongdoing. But that wasn't necessary and I later learned that I needed to be content knowing that I had an opportunity to voice my opinion. On the bright side, I was able to express my frustrations without cursing or make threats. That was an improvement from not too long before when I couldn't contain my anger enough to not get kicked out of my aunt and uncle's home. In tough situations, I had always been very reactive and unable to control my emotions. Realizing that I was making progress, I felt better immediately.

This incident also helped me take a look at myself in the mirror. I was able to reflect on situations where I may have caused poor outcomes with patients when that could have been avoided. The rude nurse wasn't the only one acting this way. Prior to taking time to reflect on these situations, I had always justified belittling behaviors as "part of the job." Sadly, it was more like a power trip, and admitting that to myself was hard.

So hard that I made the decision to be more consciously aware of my interactions with patients and families, while working harder to help them feel supported and empowered. That was a difficult task to do, considering I hadn't grown up with that type of support. It became important to me, however, because I knew what it felt like. Just like a child who grew up with an alcoholic father and despised alcohol, I also did not want to be the cause of unnecessary pain. I reminded myself every day to heighten my awareness of my surroundings every time I had the opportunity to affect patients' lives.

Instead of walking around with my head down documenting the presence of live bodies, I would look up from my clipboard as much as possible to smile and ask people how they were. I wasn't a therapist or nurse at the time, so it wasn't officially my job to ask patients their thoughts. Despite this, I developed a genuine interest. Not everyone was willing to engage in small talk, but most people seemed to like it. At first, I was silently offended when someone ignored me or brushed me off as an annoyance. It played into my own self-esteem issues, especially when that person presented himself or herself as the typical bully. But after a while, I learned to not take it personally.

Taking the time to get to know our patients helped me view them as people. You see, patients don't really have many humanistic features. They become names labeled with numbers that are placed in a treatment funnel and expected to follow a prescribed plan. Somewhere in this funnel, their number becomes a small part of an accounting flow sheet. Oftentimes, employees who have never interacted with a patient in a clinical setting make the decision as to whether or not that number's physical or emotional ailments justify dollars spent on care. People, on the other hand, have hopes, dreams, goals, disappointments, and a life that is abruptly disrupted by whatever caused their hospitalization. Seeing them as people, rather than patients, helped me see that I was a lot like them.

I remember one patient in particular who had always slightly frightened me. I had heard the nurses discuss this woman, describing her as having multiple personalities. I honestly didn't have a clue what that meant, so my judgment of this woman was based solely on the negative vibes that I felt from some of the nurses. A few times, I overheard someone expressing their frustration with this specific woman being a chronic patient who seemed to rotate through the "revolving doors" of the psych unit. She seemed depressed all of the time and often displayed extreme emotions. One minute she might be smiling, and the next she might be on the floor curled up in a ball screaming with a whimpering voice, "Stop! Stop! Please Stop!" I assumed she was "crazy" and a lost cause and her childish demeanor caused me to assume she wasn't very smart.

All of this changed when I applied my new philosophy of getting to know patients as people to the woman who I had previously avoided like the plague. I was in a particularly good mood and felt quite confident so I walked right up with a smile and pep in my step to ask her how she was. To my surprise, she answered in a calm and rational voice, "You know, I'm really struggling right now. Thank you for asking," she said. Most people in today's society get so used to asking how someone is doing without actually listening to the response. Even more people simply respond with "Good, thanks" and then both people move on without a second thought. In this moment, however, I chose to sit down next to her on the carpeted hospital floor where she was leaning against the wall in the hallway.

"What's got you down?" I asked. She proceeded to tell me about the relationships that have been crumbling in her life because of her inability to cope with the childhood trauma of being raped by her father. For 20 years, she suppressed the memories to finish college, get married, start a career, and raise two children. Her children were about my age, the youngest only just moving away to college. She had become an empty nester. I'm sure that the empty-nest syndrome is difficult for any parent; but for her it was much more. She had kept herself busy by making the role of taking care of her children her sole purpose and focus. She found her identity in them, working every day of her life to make sure that they were protected and cared for. With the children out of the house, she no longer had the everyday distraction. As a result, her repressed memories started to come back. Her husband didn't know how to deal with her newly surfaced emotional instability, so he left her as well. Her entire world crumbled before her, leaving her with nothing more than her thoughts, memories, and childhood trauma. This long list of stressors now had ample real estate in her brain to replay over and over. They became so bad that sometimes she actually felt like he was still on top of her. Just as it was impossible to get him off her when it happened, she also felt it was impossible to stop the flashbacks. As a result, she felt and reacted as if she was still 12 years old. She regressed to the age when the trauma occurred and she was stuck at this age when she was overwhelmed because she had not been able to address what had happened. This is a common thing that happens to trauma survivors.

Her multiple psychiatric admissions were a desperate attempt to prevent her from killing herself because she often felt that she couldn't live with the flashbacks. To top it all off, she was deathly afraid of losing her relationships with her children due to the instability that she had brought to their lives. There was a reason behind her "crazy" attitude that I could have never imagined. I felt like a complete jerk for previously judging her instead of taking the time to get to know her. In a matter of minutes, this patient became a person who had feelings that I not only cared about, but also could relate to. I truly believe that if more people take the time to simply listen after asking how someone is, a workplace, community, and entire culture could transform. It is possible to make the world a happier place.

That same week I was able to meet her two children. After spending only five short minutes talking with her son, I could tell he felt a lot like I did. He wanted nothing but the best for his mother and drove back from college twice per month to support her. He and his sister would spend time with her even when she was in a locked psychiatric unit, and the drugs had her so sedated that she could barely hold a conversation. It was as if I was staring in the mirror and my relationship with my mother was staring back at me. Watching them interact was one of the biggest blessings I could have ever asked for, but never would have. It was too close to home for me to feel comfortable admitting that I could relate to their family struggles. I felt much safer observing from the distance of a white coat and clipboard.

Sometimes it is hard to see the forest through the trees. That is a statement that rings true for many things, and at that time, it was very true for my life and relationships with my family members. All I knew was that I hated how I felt when I watched my mother, sister, and nephew live unhappy and unfocused lives, lives that appeared to lack passion and purpose. I also knew the way I felt when I used to live with my mother in middle school; I simply felt unsafe. The extremes of emotions I battled with, the empty cupboards, the strange men, the time spent alone seeking attention in the neighborhood that led to getting my nose broken by older kids, joining another group of older kids to steal; none of it felt right. But I did it because doing anything felt better than doing nothing, alone. When I did spend time with my mother in our trailer, it often resulted in screaming matches. A few times in middle school, it escalated to physical altercations.

I remember one time specifically where my mother was attempting to force me to do something. I don't remember what it was; all I remember was that I didn't feel safe with the situation. I decided it was time for me to leave for a while to cool down, but she trapped me on the couch. I pushed her away as strong as I could and went for the door. Before I got there, she caught me again and attempted to restrain me from leaving. I know in my heart that she was not intending to beat me or hurt me, but with as intense as the situation had become, her arm was around my chest and close to my neck, I panicked.. I bit her as hard as I could and bolted out of the trailer. When I came back later in the evening, there was a deputy sheriff at the house waiting to talk to me. He very firmly scolded me for abusing my mother and informed me that she could press charges for assault and have me sent to a "jail for kids." He also made sure to point out that if I was older, he wouldn't hesitate to lock me up for leaving a bite mark on my mother. Not one time did he talk to me privately to ask me what had happened, if I felt safe, or why I bit my own mother.

These were the types of memories that replayed in my brain. Even though I wasn't living through it anymore my heart would still race when I thought about it. I never understood why we lived like that when I was younger I just knew that I didn't like it so I never gave it much thought; it was too painful. This made it very difficult for me to see the forest through the trees. I was so focused on my own pain that I never considered the pain of others until I took the time to get to know this woman, who once frightened me, and her children.

Critical Thinking Moment: Have you ever experienced a time when your pain was so intense that you couldn't, or wouldn't, see the other person's point of view? Although your frustration and anger may be justified, refusing to see the other person's point of view prevents a deeper level of understanding. The most important aspect of learning to be an overcomer, rather than just a survivor, is understanding.

I think it was important that I got to know her perspective before meeting her children. Had I met her children first, I probably would have felt their pain so much that it would have tainted my view of their mother. In turn, this would have reinforced the negative feelings associated with my own mother. Fortunately, that's not how it happened. Getting to know her first was like getting to know my own mother with an empathetic viewpoint without ever having to be face-to-face with her. I realized that my mother's extreme emotions and inability to provide a healthy, functioning household when I was younger stemmed from her own traumatizing experiences, just like this woman's did. It didn't make my negative childhood experiences "okay," but it made me feel okay about my mom. There was a point when I felt like giving up on having a relationship with her, but putting two and two together made me a lot more understanding of her journey and our journey as a family. With this understanding, I knew that I would never be able to give up on her. That didn't fix our relationship, but with that understanding I was able to feel safe in having her back in my life. It had to be done with specific boundaries, but I never thought it would be possible.

I believe that if you seek a deeper understanding of the other person in any relationship, establishing healthy boundaries for how to keep that person in your life, then you are less likely to lose the important attachments that keep you grounded in your identity. There will always be people who are not meant to be in your life, while others are meant to be in your life for a season. Never allow a lack of understanding to cause you to lose the relationships that have shaped who you are. You won't be able to save all of them, but at least be able to stare yourself in the mirror and know you gave it your best.

The important attachments that keep you grounded in your identity. There will always be people who are not meant to be in your life, while others are meant to be in your life for a season. Never allow a lack of understanding to cause you to lose the relationships that have shaped who you are. You won't be able to save all of them, but at least be able to stare yourself in the mirror and know you gave it your best.

ALWAYS ASK "WHY?"

*"...behaviors, attitudes, and actions that
decrease an individual's ability to maintain a
feeling of safety, security, and happiness."*

A s a speaker who shares intimate details of my life struggles and how I overcame them to be happier and more successful, people who follow my online presence, or have been in my audiences, often reach out to me for advice. I receive emails and Facebook messages on a weekly basis asking for "how-to" tips for breaking through barriers in their lives. I once heard that, as humans, we are very social creatures, craving human connection. With that in mind, it makes sense that most of the problems that people come to me with are related to relationships. Usually all of the issues I write about are issues that I have either dealt with myself or have been very close to with family members or previous clients. I always do research and talk with mentors before responding to these very sensitive subjects. That is imperative, especially when these articles occasionally end up published in an online magazine.

Sometimes the questions come from young men struggling to get along with their parents, while others come from parents or professionals dealing with difficult situations with their biological, foster, or adoptive children. Many times, the questions come from young women ages 16-24 and sometimes the questions address a topic that I've never really thought about before. All of the questions, however, share similarities. Each of them stems from the desire to have a deeper understanding of human interaction. Here is a brief list of some of the questions I have received within a few months of publishing this book:

-"I'm a social worker now, but I can't stop being afraid that my friends or guys I date will not like something I say and leave me. I'm supposed to help others, but I can't help myself. How do I overcome my fear of abandonment?"
-"How do I deal with my overbearing mom?"
-"How do I leave an abusive relationship?"
-"How do I overcome my anxiety?"
-"How do I handle big changes? I have a great opportunity, but what if it doesn't work? What if I fail?"

Some of the problems I am asked to help with might seem trivial, while others are situations that may be a life or death scenario for that person. I can't think of one suicide threat that I reported to as a Crisis Worker that did not have relationship problems at the core of its existence. If you take a look at some of your own problems in life, my guess is that you'll probably identify specific relationship interactions that have caused these problems. More often than not, these problems likely stem from actions or behaviors demonstrated by other humans in your life that created a negative experience, or ongoing situation, that you now have to cope with.

Even internal battles that may not seem to be related to relationship problems usually are. Upon first glance, the above question related to handling "big changes" seems unrelated to relationships. Yet, after reading more about that person's explanation for why he was struggling, it was obvious that the struggle had its roots in previous relationship experiences. Remember the hypothetical 16-year-old girl mentioned in the introductory chapter? Like her, this man dealt with several traumatizing experiences that impacted his thoughts and behaviors related to his willing to relocate and leave what he is familiar with for the opportunity to have something better. He couldn't stop imagining the worst outcomes that were possible in his life.

The slow process of having his self-esteem beaten down by his parents who discouraged risk-taking and constantly warned him of the potentially horrible results of failing was emotionally traumatizing to him. He was unable to view his parents as supportive, and this made it impossible for him to feel secure in his own decision-making. After taking a serious look at what the worst outcome might be, he was able to see that the negative "what if the sky is falling" attitude he shared made the potentially devastating outcome seem much worse than it actually would be. Coming to this realization helped him understand that his parents' cynical outlook on life had a very detrimental impact on his own perspectives.

He was then able to rationally analyze the cost-to-benefit ratio of making the move, or not. After making a list of all of his positive qualities, such as having a college degree, with an already established skill set, he decided to take the risk. Even if he made the big move and his opportunity fell through, he still had what it would take to be able to get another job. At least he would not end up homeless or begging for money to catch a bus back to mommy and daddy. He decided that if roughing it for a week until his parents could send him money was the worst possible situation, then it probably isn't as bad as he thought. Understanding why he had such an extreme fear of failure allowed him to set a plan, make the move, and have a much happier life.

Working in the mental health unit as a psychiatric technician gave me my first exposure to the importance of understanding the "why" behind behaviors. As you may recall from the previous chapter, understanding how the generational cycles of neglect and abuse impacted my mother, this helped me be more at peace with her behaviors that impacted my childhood. The progress that I made from observing another family, as if I was "staring in the mirror," helped me begin the process of understanding the why behind many of my own behaviors. The biggest issue for me has always been romantic relationships.

I always craved having supportive and empowering relationships in my life. I wanted to be close to my mother, sister, and father more than anything. Since I did not receive that, I became very independent. I also became very protective over my emotions. Some people say it is good to "guard your heart." Well, after being burned a few times by my own family, and a romantic relationship that made me wonder why love exists, I built a fortress around my heart. It was guarded by manipulation as well as placing judgment on others, especially potential romantic relationship partners.

I would often look for any excuse to say that a girl was "not marriage material." This could have been anything from having toes that were the "wrong shape" to not having a career that was ambitious enough. Never mind the fact that she might be a doctor who enjoys traveling and wine tasting. Or that she enjoys exercising with me and has a very healthy and supportive family. If a dating relationship appeared to take a turn towards having a significant attachment, I would bolt in the other direction. Somewhere, very deep inside of me, I had a gut feeling that leading women on wasn't right. That bad feeling made it difficult for me to break up with every one of the women who eventually wanted something "more." Instead, I would find a way to make them happy they got rid of me. It wasn't too difficult to pin-point what might be a "deal-breaker" for a woman, and act it out. But not one time was it something that I would normally do. I felt very out of character capitalizing on deal-breakers, but I felt at least that it helped them move on from our connection without having to make them feel not wanted. Instead, I just looked like a jerk.

It felt horrible. Every. Single. Time. You'd think I would have learned, but all through my 20's, I avoided the thoughts, feelings, and pains related to building and breaking emotional bonds. I replaced them with a large dose of casual sex. I started using casual sex as a way to look cool to my buddies when I was younger. Bringing a different girl home every night was one of the ways that I would seek attention from my peers, especially between the ages of 18 and 21. I didn't know how to develop friendships in a healthy manner, so I used what I could. After a while, I noticed some of my friends settling into fulfilling relationships and being very happy without casual sex. It wasn't as cool as the rap videos that I watched made it seem. It didn't take long before the showboating of attractive trophies turned to sneaking women around my college fraternity house, hoping nobody would notice. It was especially embarrassing when the women I was sneaking in were not women I found attractive. If I were to describe how it felt, I would say that it made me feel sad, lonely, and shameful. The sex would mask the shame temporarily, but it would come back worse every time. Through my health care career, I have found there are many more men who live like this than I could have ever imagined.

You might be thinking, "mommy issues," and I must agree. For the longest time, I was blind to the fact that these issues had anything to do with the less than fulfilling relationship that I had with my family. When well-intending dating partners brought it to my attention, I would flat out refuse to accept it. I didn't believe that it was possible that my behaviors were associated with my childhood, or current discontent with familial relationships. I actually thought there were many things wrong with the majority of girls I dated or slept with. That all changed when I read one very special book. Ironically, my own biological mother gave this special book to me as a gift, shortly after my 30th birthday.

The book is called Attached: The New Science of Adult Attachment and How It Can Help You Find - and Keep - Love. It was truly mind-blowing for someone like myself who has struggled with intimate relationships my entire life. The advice that I have shared from this book with friends and colleagues has proven just as effective, even for individuals who generally have established healthy relationships. My favorite take-away from the book was the comparison and contrasting of the three different types of attachments. It was described on a spectrum. For simplicity, you might want to view it as the extremes of political parties. The far left is the "anxious" attachment. The far right is the "avoidant" attachment. Sitting right in the middle is the "secure" attachment. The anxiously attached relationship partner is always craving to be validated by the partner. The avoidant relationship partner tends to give just enough to get what they want in the relationship and then backs off saying, "I need space," whereas the secure relationship partner can be content in whom they are, without the need to pull someone too close (anxious) or push someone away after they get too close (avoidant). Throughout the book, psychiatrist and neuroscientist Dr. Amir Levine and Rachel Heller describe the core connection between my avoidance behaviors and my lack of secure relationships in my childhood. The complexities that I faced throughout my lifetime were simplified in a very easy to understand format. Honestly, I was surprised that I had never come across this information in my studies or career experiences before. I had a general idea of the principle of avoidant behaviors, but had never applied them to my life. Gaining a deeper understanding has helped me improve the way that I think and feel in any relationship in my life. If you ever feel like you don't understand a relationship partner's behaviors, I encourage you to read even just the first 5 chapters of the book Attached. This book helped me understand that grasping the why behind my own behaviors is only one part of the picture. The other part is understanding and appreciating other people's journeys.

My job as a mental health crisis worker reinforced this knowledge. It also reinforced the importance of treating the root cause of behaviors, also known as "symptoms," as opposed to masking them, much as I did through self-soothing with casual sex. Unfortunately, this also made me aware that the mental health system that is supposed to help people often re-traumatizes individuals through covering up symptoms, rather than treating the cause of the symptoms. Although I could identify several case studies that would highlight how "the system" often inhibits mental and emotional growth, I need not look further than my own mother.

The relationship between my mother and me is one that is a continual source of pain, stress, and opportunity. In the previous chapter, I ended with the encouragement to never give up on loved ones. I stress this because it is something that I personally struggle with, to this very day. I try very hard to hear my mother out, and to be open to any potential rekindling of that relationship. In no way do I strive to belittle or blame her for my own misfortune. Indeed, many of the decisions that she made during my childhood impacted my emotional wellness. At the same time, I have worked to understand where she is coming from.

My mother has come a long way since the traumatizing experiences that set her down the path of re-creating negative generational cycles with my sister and me. She has been on her own journey of overcoming, and I try very hard to respect that. Often times, she expresses to me that she does not feel that I "know the whole story." It is like she wants so deeply for me to understand the why behind what happened in my childhood. I listen to every word she says and I don't blame her for it. Sometimes, I wish she could accept my understanding, but I feel like it is a continual uphill battle. I don't want to make assumptions, but my observation is that my futile attempts to give her my forgiveness are a direct result of extreme shame. She wasn't able to give me what I needed, even though giving her children what they needed was the most important thing to her. Her heart was in the right place, but she did not have the tools or resources to carry out her heart's desire.

Critical Thinking Moment: Is there a relationship in your life that could benefit from a deeper level of understanding, from either side? What do you think it would take for you to understand them more, or for them to understand you more? Keep in mind that sometimes acceptance for the other person and their views, can be even more powerful than understanding.

One of the most powerful things my mother has shared with me about her experience of "traveling into, through, and out of America's mental health system" is a profound one. She has told me several times that when she went to the doctors for help, she was in distress. Her marriage had fallen apart, she had lost her job, and she was an emotional wreck. Instead of viewing her erratic behaviors as normal reactions to very abnormally stressful life situations, they were viewed as "symptoms" and labeled with a psychiatric diagnosis. During her first placement in a mental health unit, they placed her on multiple psychotropic medications, which impaired her cognitive ability to function. The side effects worsened her symptoms, and she was given more medications to mask the side effects. At the time, she was uneducated on how to regulate her emotions during trivial times. She trusted "the doctors," yet the doctors masked the symptoms with pills and created different symptoms. Never once was she educated on cognitive behavioral approaches to altering behavior patterns. Not once was she validated during her distressful times. Not once did someone ask "why?" These may seem like drastic claims to make, but as a previous crisis worker, I observed this pattern many times.

Throughout my career, I have met great people who identify as "bipolar" or are labeled with "schizoid personality disorder," amongst an array of other diagnoses such as schizophrenia, borderline personality disorder, and ADHD. When I ask them, "How long have you been diagnosed?" some of them say "forever" and they often give me an age like, "since I was 12."

Many people place judgment upon these individuals at this point, and see them as permanently damaged with a life sentence of living in chaos due to the many labels in the mental health system. Even worse, many of the diagnosed individuals place their identity in "being" a label/diagnosis. I feel that this places them at risk for discrimination, as a result of the negative stigma associated with mental health diagnoses.

As a registered nurse, I find it is no surprise that one might find their identity in a diagnosis. This sense of identity is fully supported by the medical model of health care that is, all-too-often, inappropriately utilized in mental health services. For example, if you are a type 1 diabetic that is something that you cannot control, for the most part. A doctor can label an incurable illness, or disease, and the patient receives an answer to the questions, "What's wrong with me?" with a plan of care. There is never a need to ask "Why?" because there is nothing we can change to reverse or "heal" the illness.

When you fail to ask yourself, "why?" then you fail to address the root problem of whatever is causing negative behaviors in your life. When you pass judgment on other people's behaviors, you fail to reach a deeper understanding of why and miss many great opportunities in those relationships. We need to remember that a mental health diagnosis is nothing more than a description of symptoms. Such symptoms are generally a list of behaviors, attitudes, and actions that decrease an individual's ability to maintain a feeling of safety, security, and happiness.

When someone tells me that they were diagnosed at age 12, I simply ask "Why?" Most of the time they are shocked by the question, as no one has ever taken the time to listen. They usually struggle to offer a response. At that time, I re-phrase the question by asking, "What happened when you were 12?" I have not done extensive trials or studies on this, but for three years I specifically focused on asking "why" or "what happened" in my work as a crisis worker and 100% of the time they give me a very direct answer. For example, "I was beaten and raped by my dad when I was 12" or "I didn't have parents and my only family was my grandma, and she died then."

Instead of avoiding the difficult topics their answers presented, I offered validation. I utilized the active listening skills discussed in chapter 4. I then helped them understand that they are not "crazy," as many first thought they were. I would literally tell them, "No, I don't think you're crazy. I don't know one person who could make it through your situation without doing the same thing" and I meant it. Having spent much of their lives finding their identity in mental health diagnoses, most of them felt relieved to simply not feel judged in that moment. Yes, their behaviors might have warranted a "crazy" label, in the sense of abnormal behaviors, but there was always a reason behind them. When they were able to view their symptoms as "behaviors" that they had control over, they were able to find hope. Hope that they could be happier and healthier someday.

My mother finally found hope once she started asking, "Why?" At the time of this writing, she had been free from all psychotropic medications for five years. The pain in her voice when discussing her lengthy recovery process from going off all meds after 17 years is very disheartening. She is no longer sleeping all day, and she recovered the majority of her cognitive functioning. She has even gone back to college and joined the 2016 graduating class, working towards a double major in psychology and sociology. Such a feat seemed impossible for many years. She was told to give up hope, but fought to find answers. After finally trusting her gut instinct that "something wasn't right," she made progress and began the journey of a healthier and happier life. She was able to do so by focusing on living a mentally and emotionally balanced life, free of drugs and full of healthy foods and exercise.

There is always a reason behind behavior. Instead of giving up on any behaviors that may be impeding your happiness with yourself or your relationships, take a minute to ask "why?" and do so with an inquisitive and open mind.

⁂

Critical Thinking Moment: Have you ever felt judged when seeking counseling or therapy? How about receiving therapy that didn't seem to ever make any progress? Don't give up. Remember that therapy is nothing more than expressing ourselves while receiving feedback to help us change our own behaviors. There is no shame in it. Next time you seek a therapist, ask if they are trained in trauma informed care practices. This might help you identify the "why?"

TRUST YOUR GUT

"I gave in and took a puff..."

A t one point, I struggled daily with insecurities. So much so that I often read into even the most meaningless comment or action, and assumed that others thought the worst of me. I often questioned myself and wondered if I was on the right path. I wondered if the relationships in my life were ones that I should keep. When I saw successful people who seemed rather happy, I felt very small inside. There is no doubt in my mind that this is the result of struggling to find my identity, after once having known who I was and then having my entire life turned upside down as a child. It is astonishing how childhood events continue to impact our confidence and the way we think, act, and feel about ourselves later in life.

For the longest time, this precipitated negative self-talk suppressed my ability to trust myself. Although I still have those thoughts occasionally, they no longer prevent me from seeing my own greatness. More importantly, they no longer prevent me from trusting that I, and only I, know what's best for me. This is a far cry from the times when I once sought validation and reassurance from any person possible. I will expand more on validation in a later chapter.

My transition from debilitating negative self-talk to finding my own greatness occurred partly because I realized that I am not the only one who has such insecurities. The other part is because I learned the hard way that my internal voice is usually right. This lesson came because of many bad things happening after ignoring my own gut feelings and instincts.

I believe that every person has an internal voice guiding them, but sometimes negative experiences of our past cause that voice to be silenced and replaced with insecurities. If you have ever questioned yourself or felt "not good enough," I'm sure you can relate. If you are someone who tends to be very confident, I encourage you to use this chapter as a reminder of the times when you have doubted your greatness. We can all use this as a reminder to be sensitive to our friends, family members, and co-workers who likely struggle with trusting themselves in certain aspects of life and decision-making. It never hurts to be more aware and supportive of those around you.

As a public speaker and health care professional, hundreds of people every year open up to me, not because I am anything special, and not because of my education, but because I remain open, as well. This does not mean that I expose every detail of my past traumatizing experiences, but when I feel that someone is struggling, I will share small bits of my own struggles. This lets them know that their insecurities are safe with me. My demeanor and compassion show that I feel where they are coming from, even if I've never been where they are. If you are someone who is capable of showing extreme empathy, you probably know the feeling I am talking about. That's exactly what it is, a feeling, not a word or description.

Whether I am on stage or in a hospital room, I remain open and transparent as much as possible. Sometimes I'm just not up to it, but I still try. I welcome people's connections and have a genuine interest in their thoughts. This often leads to them divulging significant personal information, at times, excessively. Sometimes it is relevant to the reason we are talking, but usually it is completely irrelevant. They sense empathy and jump at the opportunity to expose their darkest secrets with someone who feels "safe," without being judged. If only they knew the countless individuals who do the same. Maybe they wouldn't feel so alone. Maybe this section will be helpful to you, as well. Knowing that many more people than you might have dark secrets could be relieving, if you have your own. I personally feel a little better each time I give advice to someone who comes to me with a problem that I have recently struggled with. I am grateful that they had the courage to open up to me. When that happens, not only do I receive an opportunity to help them, but I often find that I have had similar issues. It feels good to know that you're not alone in struggling with certain behaviors or past experiences that you generally bottle up as secrets.

It is quite often that I hear about other people's deepest fears and struggles, ranging from childhood molestation and teen prostitution to infidelity and suicidal thoughts. Week after week, over a decade of working in health care and mental health services showed me that thousands of people have the same exact self-defeating thoughts that I had, and sometimes still do. I believe that everyone struggles with insecurities at times. Some people allow these insecurities to show, while others hide them quite well.

Critical Thinking Moment: Have you ever allowed your insecurities to show? It is important to know when it is okay to let them show and when it is not appropriate. It will mostly depend on how comfortable you feel exposing a side of you that most people don't see. Be sure to choose wisely. Keep in mind that even though it may be uncomfortable, being vulnerable is a key aspect of learning to understand and overcome.

I have had clients who were CEOs of multi-million dollar companies, but had never overcome the traumatic experiences of their past. Although they seem intimidating and untouchable to their employees, deep inside they were struggling with the very idea of trusting themselves. When something traumatizing happens, such as a death in the family, a significant financial loss, or relationship issues, these people respond the same way as you and me. They are traumatized. They have the same self-defeating thoughts and consider giving up. They would often be very careful about who they "broke down" around and would ask certain people to leave if it might impact their credibility as a leader.

During my time with them, these CEOs needed to be reminded of their greatness, just as you and I do. Reminding them of how great they were, despite their circumstances, is really all I did. It was easy for me to see how great they were from the outside, but nearly impossible for them to grasp while in crisis. When their lives seemed to be crumbling around them, it made it very difficult to trust their own decisions. For the most part, they usually still had the capacity to make good life decisions, but they just couldn't trust themselves at that moment in time. Realizing that even the people who I once saw as rocks, those that would never bend or break, struggled with the same insecurities as I did, I found it very reassuring. Oftentimes, they even exposed many of the poor decisions that they had made in the past. That helped me build the confidence to be able to share my own bad decisions in this next story. I learned to trust my gut, the hard way.

Battling with my own insecurities and self-doubt didn't truly start to go away until my mid-to-late 20's. I know there are many people who take on that daily battle for much longer than I, even for an entire lifetime. I am thankful that I have found a path of self-actualization and improved self-esteem. Still, it has impacted my relationships and decision- making, but not nearly to the detriment that it did during my high school and college years.

Because of this, I tended to generally keep to myself. It wasn't difficult, considering I lived on a farm with my aunt and uncle while in high school.

Ironically, all through college, I lived in a social fraternity. I spent most of my time finding excuses to avoid gatherings that required small talk or "normal" conversations where other guys would discuss friendships, family, or anything else that made me uncomfortable. The few times that I did attempt to partake in those conversations generally resulted in my being questioned about topics, like why I stayed on campus working during holiday breaks instead of going "home." I didn't really feel like I had a home to go to during breaks, which is a common issue with college students who come from broken homes or foster care. Other popular questions revolved around the fact that I was viewed as "crazy." I really can't blame them, and I truly identified with that persona at the time. I was willing to do anything to get a rush, show off, and simply be recognized for being good at something, or having cool experiences to share, even if those experiences were dangerous or illegal. My peers would show an interest in the wild things that I did, and I would eagerly tell them about it just to later realize that they were only interested because they can't believe someone would do such idiotic things. These "things" ranged from stealing, to picking a fight with a drunk guy twice my size. I was known for developing ideas like going to the "hood" and breaking into buildings, purely for the rush.

Bouncing back and forth from being a "normal" student with a job to being a thief was a skill that I later self-labeled as being a chameleon. This skill is a direct result of survival instincts. The same instincts that once allowed me to leave a boardroom, go to a hood-rat house in the slums and, in the same suit pants, write slam poetry and drink 40 ounce bottles of Old English. Around those neighborhoods this succulent malt liquor has earned the nickname O-E, one of the many terms that occasionally slipped out of my mouth in the wrong company. In chapter 7, this chameleon lifestyle is described as operating from "two screens."

I remember one cold winter night in Iowa when I had the unfortunate pleasure of meeting a former superstar linebacker from the local university. We met in the wee hours of the morning. I had spent all Friday night attempting to make friends with a new group of people who, like me, were interested in writing and recording hip-hop and R&B songs. I thought it would be cool to connect with other like-minded people in hopes that they might accept my self-proclaimed outcast persona, one that happened to include being a white rapper who listened to 2pac gangster rap every day. Sadly, they ended up being a very bad group of people. I was seeking acceptance so blindly that I allowed myself to fall victim to peer pressure.

I never did drugs. Actually, due to watching both my mother and sister suffer horribly, and nearly dying as a result of street drugs, prescription drugs, or a combination of the two, I despised drugs. But my desire to fit in and make music seemed to take over.

I had connected with this group through a social web site where people could share music. It was mostly garage bands and amateur hip-hop artists looking to "get discovered" using their 20 dollar mic and 10 dollar headphones from the Wal-Mart electronic section. One of the guys in this group sent me a house address to join them that Friday night. I eagerly pulled out my special baggy jeans that I thought would make me look more like a rapper, put on a hat tilted to the side (I never usually wore hats) and drove to the address using a printed MapQuest map to navigate. I wasn't familiar enough with the city to realize this house was in the wrong part of town.

It was a dirty house with shaggy brown marble-colored carpet that appeared to be still in place from 1971. The living room was so small that the 12 hopeful rappers holding marijuana filled blunts, Black & Mild cigars, and brown paper bags filled with booze took up most of the walking space. The rest of the room was filled with several large speakers that were hooked up to the ancient boom box that was somehow wired to the cream-colored IBM computer that probably still used dial-up. I found an open spot on the dirty, green, fake, leather couch and squeezed in between two guys who were much larger and more street savvy than myself. I wondered when we were going to start making hit records that would be played on the radio. Instead, what was actually happening was that people with no plans for their future were smoking, drinking, and performing freestyle rap lyrics, also known as "spitting freestyles." These lyrics lacked originality and talent, and they were using what I would say was, at best, mediocre audio equipment.

After refusing to participate multiple times, I gave in and took a puff from the weed pipe that was getting passed around the room. I knew that something didn't feel right, yet I also didn't have enough self-respect to follow my gut instinct and simply leave. I wondered, "What if they could give me what I need and want in friendship?" I thought it might be a chance to not feel so alone. I suddenly understood why many very lost individuals often resort to gang membership.

Within five minutes of smoking whatever they were passing around, I was actively hallucinating. The room was spinning and appeared to be getting smaller. I started to worry that they might be planning to do something to me. I'm pretty sure you could call that chemically-induced paranoia. It took that level of extreme paranoia to get me to leave the place that I probably shouldn't have been at anyway. Since I had never been an active drug user, I was not familiar with what was happening to me. It was scary.

As I was driving down the road shortly afterward, I saw what seemed to be trees growing out of the street. I drove five miles per hour clenching the steering wheel. My eyes felt like they were going to pop out of their sockets as I tried to reason with myself that it was not possible that a tree was actively growing out of concrete. I approached the tree and, thankfully, it disappeared when I drove through it.

I didn't want to go back to the fraternity house where my peers were likely having normal social interactions, playing poker, and drinking beer with people they trusted. Instead, I went to a place where I felt more comfortable, a small dance club on the east side of town where I was always the only white male. The vibe of the east side was often said to be similar to that of "south-side Chicago." There had been at least one drive by shooting at this club within the past six months. A good friend of mine, Dante, later wrote a song about a drive by shooting at the same club. When I became an ER nurse in that same city, I later wrote a song about taking care of the young gang members who came in with bullet wounds, and scalps that had been cracked open by broken beer bottles. But when I was 19, none of the shootings or fights seemed to matter.

This club served me underage because I knew the DJ. I once recited some of my rhymes for him and he said, "It was pretty good, but keep trying." I thought he would tell me it sucked, so I took that as a compliment and kept bringing him more music to listen to. I think he was too nice to tell me how horrible it was. I guess it didn't matter to me; as long as when I went to the club, he called the security guards off if they harassed me. Later in life, I ran into that same DJ and ended up hiring him to DJ some of my live events, both for hip-hop shows and speaking in schools. I think he might actually like my music now that I share some of these stories of overcoming in lyric form, instead of trying to make distasteful dance music, widely known in hip-hop and urban culture as "booty shakin' music." My baggy jeans just weren't enough to inspire the genius rap lyrics that formulate a club hit.

That night, I sat at the end of the bar writing rap lyrics and drinking Hennessy on the rocks. As I became immersed in my comfort zone, the time passed all too quickly, along with three glasses of liquor. Before I knew it, DJ Daze was on the mic saying, "You ain't gotta go home, but you gotta get the f*** outa here!" He always had a way with words. It blended perfectly with the environment and the baggy jeans that I had previously stolen from a local department store.

When I tried to pay my tab, the bar tender reminded me that I had already paid it. So, I walked out to my car and realized I had lost my keys. Frustrated and wide-eyed, I walked slowly around the club, searching in places I knew I hadn't even walked to. I couldn't believe I had lost them, so I walked back and forth a few times before thinking I found them stuck in a frozen puddle. Turns out it was just a broken piece of plastic that resembled the black grip on my car key. Feeling defeated, I reached into my back pocket to see if I had enough money for a cab and found my keys. You would think that by this time I would have recognized that I shouldn't drive. Instead, I quickly got in my car, clutched the steering wheel, and drove so slow that I could actually count the dotted lines in the passing lane.

By this time, I was no longer seeing trees growing out of the road. Naturally, I assumed that the alcohol had taken the edge off whatever I had smoked. I don't think I was quite experienced, or sober, enough to recognize that enough time had likely passed to wear off the worst of the high, or that pairing alcohol with drugs might intensify the intoxication. I later described my hallucinations to someone who had previously been an avid drug user. He informed me that it was probably weed that had been "laced" with PCP. I guess that makes sense, considering the extreme paranoia that persisted, even after I was no longer enjoying the magical tree growth.

I made it home safely. Well, I was really close to home. I was just one block from my fraternity house when I noticed a cop pull out of a gas station parking lot and start trailing me slowly. I pulled into the next parking lot, parked my car, and started walking towards the house. After I had already parked and started walking, the officer must have decided something didn't seem right. He got out of his car and started yelling, "Stop!" I don't recall him identifying himself as the police, but I'm sure he probably did. All I remember is that as soon as I heard screaming, my paranoia heightened intensely. I thought someone bad was after me and ran as if my life depended on it.

I ran next to a neighbor's fence that separated the bad guy and me. I lost him just long enough for me to cross the street and jump a fence into an apartment complex. By this time, it was nearing 3AM. I knocked on several doors and attempted to open doors in case they were unlocked. I had to find somewhere safe. One couple saw me frantically asking for help. They looked straight at me and ignored my request, jetting into and locking their apartment as fast as possible. I had nowhere to go, so I hid beneath a stairwell. From my hiding spot, I was able to look out and see five squad cars with spotlights on, rolling through the complex. I waited for what seemed like eternity. Finally, the coast was clear. There was snow on the ground, I did not have a coat and was cold, and it was time to go home.

I was so cold that I completely forgot that "bad guys" had just chased me and saw a bunch of squad cars. I started walking home when I saw the former superstar football player turned local cop. I turned to run again, but he had already spotted me and was headed in my direction. I gave up, bent to my knees, put my hands above my head, and ate snow. He wasn't happy that I had evaded him and even though I was now cooperating, I still met the ground at a much faster rate than I would have on my own accord. He was pretty nice after that. He even gave me a tip and told me that I wasn't very far over the legal limit so I should breathe really fast. Indeed, I might get lucky by the time we got to the station for the formal breathalyzer, he told me. I was so paranoid that I thought he was lying. I ended up getting booked for a DUI, blowing 0.087 when the legal limit was 0.08. Exactly 30 days later, the legal limit changed from 0.08 to 0.10. All I could think of was, "If only I had listened to my gut instinct and left that house when I knew it didn't seem right."

Not trusting my gut instinct got me in trouble many other times. Over and over again, I would repeat the same pattern. Whether it was stealing from a department store or sleeping with a woman I didn't find attractive just to avoid feeling lonely; each time I knew that it would end with me feeling guilty and ashamed. Yet, I did it anyway. If I were to reflect on why I continued such self-defeating behaviors, I would say that it boils down to two things: one is that I had not overcome the situations in my past that were traumatizing to me, the other is that I had not yet taken responsibility for what happened to me.

I wanted to avoid all feelings that made me feel bad, the way that I once did when I didn't have what I always wanted in a family. The resulting mental and emotional anguish became something I fixated on. For a long time, I accepted that as the "reason" and the "excuse," for my negative behaviors. My perception was that I could not imagine that anyone else had gone through bad things like I did, so I had a pass to do whatever I wanted.

It took a long time, but I finally realized that I was re-living my past over and over again. I hated the bad memories from my childhood, so much so that I did anything to avoid those feelings. Usually, my avoidance included risk-taking behaviors. More often than not, they were illegal, or unhealthy, and impacted my life negatively. This was a different means to the same end of unhappiness, which was exactly what I was attempting to avoid, but found over and over again. My gut instinct would tell me not to do it, but even with the knowledge that it had become my responsibility, I couldn't stop myself. I knew I shouldn't do bad things, but I didn't know what I should be doing instead, or how to do it. It was like I was living in two worlds, and couldn't get out of either.

CHAPTER 9

TWO WORLDS
DISCOVERED

"I exposed the things that I was ashamed of..."

We had just finished co-presenting to a group of foster parents, and the next day we spent all day driving to speak to a group of foster youth. That night, we were back in the hotel bar chatting about our experiences. This was the first time we had talked in depth.

We didn't know each other very well, but we did know that we both have similar passions for serving the underserved and giving hope to the hopeless. I wasn't quite sure how Dr. Gregory Keck and I originally connected. I assumed it was through mutual professional connections. To a certain extent, that is slightly accurate. However, that night, Greg shared with me that he originally learned about my work through watching a video that I created, called Voices of Youth. I had created the video just for a youth group I was working with and had no idea that it was being used in child welfare conferences, and university social work classes in more than one state. After seeing the video, he tracked down the program director, and it turned out that we did have some similar connections. It wasn't long before we scheduled speaking events. I thought that was a pretty epic story. It was one of the first times that I started to build confidence in my passion for impacting large audiences.

The video wasn't fancy, by any means. Actually, it was nothing more than a photo slideshow and some meaningful words that flashed, along with music and spoken word poetry. I created the video to highlight the importance of offering unconditional love to children in foster care. I used a poem that I wrote about a girl who struggled with never feeling at home. I then had that same girl write a poem about her struggles with missing her siblings. We recorded the poems and the recordings played over the music. The video used my life and the girl's life as examples for overcoming difficult childhoods. You can still see this video on my YouTube channel that you can link to through my web site www.TravisLloyd.net.

Greg wanted to talk about things other than the video. He wanted to know more about my childhood. I shared with him some of my past struggles. I also shared about the struggles that I still faced, even as an adult in the beginning of my career. I exposed the things that I was ashamed of, including hiding the casual sex and having been involved with theft. I explained that all through my college career, I felt like two different people.

Critical Thinking Moment: Did you know that it is normal to feel like a different person depending on where you are and who you are around? We all wear many different hats at work, school, home, and different social settings. Learning to adapt to each setting helps us be well rounded. The goal should be to be able to feel comfortable in your own skin, regardless of which hat you are wearing and where you are. Be confident in you!

On one side, I was doing what I needed to do in order to survive and live independently. I held a job, either at a nursing home or in the psychiatric unit, throughout my entire college career. I maintained a full time class load. Although I wasn't the best student, I always went to class. After class, I regularly went to work. I rarely showed up late, and definitely never called in to work. My jobs and regimented schedule gave me the stability that I so desired, and lacked, in my childhood. I was helping people every week and it made me feel good about who I was. It gave me a sense of pride.

On the other side, I maintained a life outside of work and school that made me feel shameful. In the first chapter, I mentioned that my senior year of high school was a rough transition for me. After wrestling season was over, I developed a severe case of senoritis. Not only was I drinking in the middle of the day, but I spent my evenings aimlessly driving around looking for other people to connect with who might join me in doing very stupid things like breaking into homes, jumping from rooftops, or shooting paintballs at passing cars. During one of my evening adventures, I met up with some guys who were from a rival wrestling team. They had an opportunity to make money, and I had nothing but time and a need for an adrenaline rush. I joined them in a theft ring by purchasing stolen DVD players and re-selling them at a higher price. I heard that they also dealt in other items such as big screen TV's, but I kept to the small stuff. After getting rid of one round of DVD players, I was eager to find more buyers and make more cash. I called them up and they hinted to me that the phones were tapped. I never called again, but found out later that one of them had gone to prison for a 10 year sentence. I saw a photo of him on Facebook for the first time shortly after my 10-year high school reunion. That scared me for a while, but didn't keep me away for long.

More opportunities kept coming up. I became the epitome of an opportunist. I never really had the ideas, but my lack of moral judgment, low self-esteem, and desire to be accepted led me into the arms of the people who did. One of the LPN's (Licensed Practical Nurse) that I worked with in the nursing home during my freshman year of college was one of the first with her arms out. She, and her cousin, brought me in on a theft ring that targeted a clothing department store. Upon recalling this story, I believe they were both originally from South-Side Chicago. They had re-located to Iowa because they wore out their welcome in the Illinois welfare system. She worked, received child support, drove a brand new SUV, and still managed to collect food stamps. She also had a very clever idea for making money from high dollar stores.

The two of them would get dressed up really fancy, like they were shopping with lots of money to spend. When walking around the store, they would brush up against expensive items, usually small items such as high quality bras and underwear. The items would nonchalantly fall into their oversize handbags, undetected by security cameras. Then, they would simply walk out of the store. I would be waiting in the car and we would drive to the next city that had the same department store. That's where my role came in. I became "the innocent looking white boy who is returning things for his mom." It worked.

Time and time again, they would steal and I would return. Upon returning the items, without a receipt, I would be given a gift receipt as store credit. We would then purchase items with the gift receipts. When the new items were purchased, the customer service representatives would provide a new receipt that reflected it as a "cash" deal. We would then take the newly purchased items and go to yet another store, where they would gladly accept the returns and offer cash refunds.

This same nurse also had me stealing liquor from grocery

stores. I had seen someone do it once, so I didn't think much of it. The liquor that I provided was then used to sell mixed drinks at after parties. I just thought it was cool that I got to go to the after parties. The experience both fulfilled the adrenaline junkie in me and helped me feel like I was involved in something bigger than myself. If only I had paid attention to the very quiet gut feelings that told me I was being used.

After sharing some of these stories with Greg, I was anticipating being judged and shamed. Instead, he looked at me with a smile that made me feel proud of who I was. He calmly stated, "It is really amazing how you have been able to compartmentalize your lives." I was unsure of what he meant, but soon realized that after hearing my stories for only the first time, Dr. Keck was able to pinpoint something very profound. He went on to explain the psychology behind how I unconsciously functioned in Survival Mode while going through the motions of improving my life. He pointed out that I improved through education, career advancement, and stable relationships, before even knowing how to make the most of them. Dr. Keck described this as running two computer screens at the same time.

CHAPTER 10

"TWO SCREENS"

A DICHOTOMY

by Dr. Gregory Keck

"...the traumatized child may misinterpret what they perceive on their screens."

Everyone has a blueprint from early in his life-including, in utero experiences. That initial blueprint is everlasting-regardless of what transpires subsequent to its being put in place. Given the jargon of today one could replace blueprint with the first screen that was developed and opened. This foundational screen serves to provide the individual with information about his life; it gives feedback, direction, and insights. The longer the individual is alive, the more screens get developed and opened so what occurs is that the older a child gets, the more complex his development becomes. However, if trauma has interfered significantly, his developmental processes may get interrupted, reframed, diluted, compromised, and distorted. As a result, *the traumatized child may misinterpret what they perceive on their screens.*

Most of us have a default screen, and it is, in most cases, the first screen that we had. We come to rely on this screen frequently, and even when it fails to serve us well, trauma experiences cause us to trust it; that occurs because that screen may have served the person well at the time it was developing, but if the child no longer lives in the environment where those early experiences happened, he probably does not need it any longer. Though, the many moves from foster home to foster home probably eroded the formation of new functional screens. The old tapes play on while new information may be unclear and certainly, not securely stored.

As people get older, they get better at consolidating informational input they have received from their experiences, and if they can distill information from new and positive sources, they may be able to mitigate some of the primordial information they have stored in that first blueprint. If an individual's capacity to integrate new information has been somehow impaired, his default may continue to pop up to provide them with old information.

People accommodate to their trauma in many ways. Some people remain stuck in the 'old stuff'-forever, and these are the individuals who, in all probability, will continue to have a pattern of dysfunctional behavior. They, also, are the people who may continue the intergenerational transmission of trauma when they have children of their own as they haven't opened another screen with new information on it. These are the individuals who probably will have developed various kinds of personality disorders which are extremely resistant to change. The three most common personality disorders seen in people who have experienced early childhood maltreatment and have not overcome the consequences of those traumatic experiences are Borderline, Anti-Social, and Narcissistic Personality Disorders. Each of these disorders makes typical parenting highly unlikely as they will not have developed empathy which is essential for successful, effective, and nurturing parenting. One needs to keep this is mind- probably every person who causes trauma in a child's life has had their own history of early trauma, however, most people who have had early trauma DO NOT end-up being child abusers. This dichotomy is important to recall because to assume that all people who have had childhood trauma will become abusers is FALSE. It's similar to saying that it is probably true that most people who have a heroin addiction started using drugs by smoking marijuana, however, what is also true is that most individuals who smoke/ smoked marijuana do not ever use heroin.

Most healthy individuals whose development was not seriously eroded by their trauma experiences will continue to mature in a typical manner; they will move from concrete thinking and rule following to abstract thinking and conscience development. They will develop: a private self-their individual uniqueness known primarily by them, a public self-which they share with others, a social self-which emerges in casual, social situations, and a professional or working self-which is seen by those in a work setting. The trauma experiences are primarily 'stored' in the private self and may be known by those in the person's intimate interpersonal relationships; it doesn't override the other selves, though, it does exist on a level which is below all of the other selves. It may emerge and 'takeover', temporarily, when seriously triggered by something which stimulates early memories or sensory responses.

Unlike those people who do not move beyond their own abuse/ neglect, there are many individuals who successfully are able to compartmentalize components of their lives. There may be room to discuss whether or not they have integrated their trauma into the more positive and successful dimensions of their lives, however, it seems to be easier to describe and understand if we think of it from the two or more open screens analogy. For people who have multiple screen activity, as stated before, the foundational screen has retained the same information that was originally stored and saved; it is permanently available to the person who has had negative experiences, and while the individual may not use it much, it may be accessed when there is either an internal or external trigger. Healthy individuals whose psychosocial development continued to become more complex subsequent to early trauma will tend to rely more on the screen that was created later in their lives.

This more recently put together screen will empower the individual to be successful; it will also be the vehicle which will propel the person to intentionally override the thoughts which may come from the foundational screen. For example, when a person who has had early trauma becomes a parent for the first time, they, initially and automatically, may rely on their foundational screen, however, the person will become aware of the old screen's information and open the other more positive screen.

Just as the title suggests, individuals can overcome the effects of trauma; that shouldn't be taken to mean that the trauma doesn't somehow have an on-going and underlying role in the person's life that experienced trauma. It may, in fact, be a driving force for their successes. People who have not experienced trauma typically have formed positive identifications with important people in their lives; people then internalize those identifications and incorporate them into an internal value system by which they judge themselves and others. In other words, their value systems are composites of those significant people in their lives. They 'take on' the qualities that were transmitted to them and adapt them to fit their lives. The integration of another's values into one's own personality leads to how one develops perceptions of their world, and helps to determine how they interact with the world.

Conversely, individuals who have experienced trauma frequently develop negative identifications with those who perpetrated their maltreatment. This does not mean that they have necessarily have negative feelings about those perpetrators but rather that they develop their internalized value systems in a manner which is opposite of what they perceive that their perpetrators would believe or do. In other words, if they have come to perceive that their father would have done something that they found distasteful, they will, almost, automatically choose to do the opposite of what they assume that their parent would have done. Therein, that is why it is called a negative identification. Negative identifications can have positive outcomes, though, it is somewhat stressful for the person to be in a state of perpetually shifting from, "that was done to me; therefore, I will do the opposite." Of course, that is not how it happens because it does not occur that consciously, however, that is the process which occurs.

The capacity to accommodate to adversity is resilience, and resilience is the condition which allows people to face what, otherwise, might be impossible for them to manage. People who have overcome trauma are, probably, more psychosocially complex than those individuals who remain stuck in their traumatic experiences.

CHAPTER 11

A ROADMAP TO SUCCESS

"...one step towards helping them move from being a "victim" to an "advocate."

D r. Keck pointed out that I somehow managed to run both my old screen and my new screen concurrently. I didn't have a clear understanding of where I was going or how I would get there, but I maintained enough resiliency to fight through whatever came my way. Now, I work passionately and diligently to help others find their way. I hope that this shows not just in my work as a speaker, author, consultant, and mentor, but also through my previous roles in health care and mental health services.

As a crisis worker, my goal was to resolve immediate conflict. I was employed by a large mental health agency, and part of our funding came from the county, so our team was mostly considered a community service. We worked in direct collaboration with law enforcement across two counties. The only time we were called to a scene was after a police officer had been there and deemed it necessary that a mental health professional be involved in the decision-making process in order to improve the outcome for all who were involved. We were strictly forbidden to arrive at a scene without an armed officer entering first. Safety first.

The most common conflict that I was called to intervene with was suicide threats and behavior issues that were often described to me as psychotic or simply "crazy" when I received a report from the dispatchers prior to my arrival at the scene. We reported to scenes anywhere and everywhere; in the woods, on the bridges, in homeless shelters, in million dollar homes. You name it, and we've probably talked someone out of suicide or provided another sort of mental health intervention there. Most people are shocked at how often such situations occur. It rarely makes the news and the social stigma related to these topics causes people to avoid the very discussion whenever possible. A very large percentage of these calls were placed by residential living facilities, otherwise known as group homes or congregate care settings.

Critical Thinking Moment: Do you have a friend or family member who has felt suicidal or struggled with extreme emotions that impaired their ability to function? Issues like depression are known as the "silent killers" for a reason. It might not be your job to be a crisis worker, but avoiding the topic never helps. Sometimes asking the tough questions is exactly what someone needs.

Historically, congregate care settings in America utilize minimal staff to supervise large groups of youth or lower-functioning adults who have all been badly traumatized. It has been my experience that the staff members are minimally educated and paid a low wage. By no means am I placing judgment on such individuals, because I was once a 17-year-old kid working in group homes, and I also made many mistakes due to immaturity, lack of experience, and inadequate education. However, I do place a significant amount of responsibility for this repeated cycle of retaining inadequately trained staff in the hands of the board members, directors, and other financial decision makers who continue to allow a low level of education and experience requirements for applicants who work with such sensitive populations. Continuing on this rant will only deter from the intention of this chapter, so I will leave that topic to your own deliberation.

Since many of these workers do not have the critical thinking skills or a trauma-informed education that would allow them to address the root cause of crisis-inducing behaviors, they are often prescribed a "crisis plan" to follow. This crisis plan is generally written by a therapist or psychologist who occasionally meets with the individual, and most often has not developed an active and engaged relationship with the person they are serving; something that many leaders in trauma informed treatment models state is the backbone of permanent progress. At the top of this plan, you will often find a "PRN" (Per Required Needs) order for an anti-anxiety or other psychotropic medication that is frequently intended to sedate the individual displaying undesired behaviors. There were many crisis plans that I reviewed that did have other non-drug interventions listed, but the under-prepared staff members rarely had the skill-set to implement such interventions and they were ignored. So, their answer for "crazy" behaviors? You guessed it, drugs. Again, I am not passing judgment, and I am certainly not generalizing. I have heard of many group living facilities that run things very well. Unfortunately, I never had the pleasure of observing such a facility, and I am simply speaking from my personal experiences, both as a professional seeking to improve outcomes and as a former youth who experienced such facilities.

Having been forced to take Ritalin as a child myself, as well as having to watch my own mother enter "zombie" mode due to being on far too many psych meds, I have always utilized meds in crisis situations only as a last resort. This made my job more difficult and time consuming, but the result was always a deeper level of understanding from the staff members, and a calm and more peaceful end to crisis for the struggling individual. Not only did this create an improved outcome for that specific incident, but it also decreased the likelihood that the same type of incident would reoccur.

When I arrived to these situations, I was often bombarded with staff members who were just as angry and displaced as the client they were complaining about. They would explain all of the bad behaviors that someone had displayed, along with how crazy and wrong that person seemed to be. Many times, the staff member would attempt to explain to me why the individual needed to be forced to be committed prior to me ever completing an assessment. Sometimes they would explain their disgust and make committal demands while standing in front of the person they were talking about, who was in obvious mental and emotional distress. I took those belittling moments as a sign of a classic "power trip," rather than a therapeutic interaction that sought to solve a problem.

I remember being a "client" myself, experiencing one of those power trips from a nurse in the pediatric psychiatric unit that I stayed in at the age of 11. When I first arrived for admission, the facility didn't have any open beds in the children's unit, so they placed me on the adolescent unit, which was generally reserved for ages 13-17. While on the adolescent unit, I felt very out of place and downright scared. All of the other patients were much older and more mature than I was. I tried hard to fit in by not showing any emotion or reacting to things. I acted like I understood everything so that I wouldn't look dumb around the older kids. I didn't smile once. After a few days, a bed opened up in the children's unit (11 and under). Being surrounded by younger children made me feel more comfortable. I got to play video games and board games and even run around playing with toy trucks. It felt kind of normal outside of the times when I had to stay awake all night so that I would be able to fall asleep the next day while they "tested my brain" with wires stuck to my head. That was a difficult one to explain to kids at school after returning a month later.

One day while I was playing with my favorite truck in the children's psych unit, I went off into my own little world. I was away from all of the other children who were running in circles with their cars and trucks, as I became oblivious to the world around me. Going off in my own little world had become my way of coping. It made me not think about how much I missed my mother or father, and for those brief moments, I didn't feel like the smelly kid in 4th grade that left school with headaches at least twice weekly in an attempt to avoid social interaction. I enjoyed my little world and kept running my truck around the tables where everyone received their meal trays before I took off trucking down the hallway where all of the children's' bedrooms were. Before I reached the end of the hall, I heard a nurse yell down at me, "Get away from there! I told you not to go down there! That is off limits!" I had been playing by myself, so I figured that she must have told a group of children not to go down the hallway and thought that I had been in that group, but I wasn't. Her stern and accusatory voice scared me and I stopped in my tracks. I told her that I didn't hear her previous instructions, and before I had a chance to comply, she responded, "That's it! Give me the truck, you're in time out!" With a firm grip on my left arm, I was escorted to the corner - a corner at the end of the hall where I had just been told not to go. Man, that was confusing. I sat on a stool facing the two white walls until I was told it was okay to join for snack time.

I was treated like a bad kid, so I felt like a bad kid and it didn't feel good. Maybe she was so used to children manipulating her that she just assumed I was doing the same. Or perhaps she had a bad day and something wasn't right in her home life. I'll never know. All I know is that she made me feel really bad by unnecessarily exercising her power over me as her "patient" through the way that she chose to speak to and about me as she walked away from my time-out spot mumbling to her co-workers. Even if I had decided to be a rebel and drive my truck down the hall intentionally, knowing that it was off limits, it was still uncalled for to talk down, talk about, or belittle, especially when dealing with sensitive populations such as those who have been traumatized by being removed from any sense of normalcy they might have once known. It is easy to become complacent and difficult to remember all of the important lessons when we are struggling. This may be common sense to many, but it is a very important reminder to all.

The nurse probably wasn't aware of the negative impact she had that still resonates in my memory to this day. In a way, I'm thankful for the experience she gave me. It has allowed me to recognize those staff members who get stuck on a power trip and approach them with kindness rather than out of spite. I also recognized that many of those behaviors are the result of a lack of awareness and understanding. The nurse didn't understand my side of the situation and wasn't willing to listen. She also wasn't aware of how her actions were perceived by those around her, and how they could have easily caused situations to worsen had she been dealing with a more reactive child. Therefore, when working as a crisis worker, I approached situations with a goal of ensuring understanding and awareness amongst all involved.

Rather than berating the staff member for inappropriate behavior or the client for theirs, I would speak to each of them individually. If the situation seemed to be excessively escalated, I would create a plan with everyone involved and then separate each individual to speak privately. If things didn't seem too out of hand, I would have an open discussion with everyone involved while mediating to ensure that each voice was heard in a fair manner.

Along with this, I would listen to each side and work to identify what they needed. What was it that the staff person needed from the situation that they weren't getting? Usually it was a matter of the client complying with rules and regulations, receiving respect, or having a sense of control in their facility. What was it that the client was needing that they weren't getting? Usually it was very similar: receiving respect and having a sense of control in their own lives. Without receiving what they each needed, it was very easy to let very simple misunderstandings turn into a major crisis. Being able to help them understand each other and the reasons why they were not getting along was very helpful, as it helped things make sense. However, that wasn't the end of it.

I would continue to seek to understand the core reason that caused the original crisis-inducing behaviors to begin with. In the earlier chapter, "Two Screens," Dr. Keck referenced this as identifying the "triggers." This term is widely used in the psychology and mental health fields across America. Identifying and understanding the triggers would often de-escalate the situation enough to where we could talk calmly without having to resort to using sedating medications which cover the problem, but don't prevent the problem from happening again. If the situation was extreme enough, and the safety of the individual or others around them was at risk, I would sometimes encourage a medication to prevent potential physical danger. Most of the time, though, I discouraged the use of meds and offered to spend time with the individual one-on-one.

The staff members would usually look at me like I was out of my mind for being willing to spend the one-on-one time that it takes to resolve an issue rather than strictly resorting to punishment. But I would simply ignore them and offer an ear to the individual in crisis in a non-threatening and welcoming way. This usually facilitated decreased anxiety and helped them feel less judged. I would ask them where their pain came from and when the behaviors started. We would discuss things that were in their control, as well as those that were out of their control. We would then focus on personal goals and create an action plan. Getting focused on personal goals sometimes helped them see how their current negative behaviors were detrimental to their future. We also focused on how the issues that triggered them might have been rather insignificant when considering the bigger picture of their life and purpose. This may seem like common sense to a lot of you reading this, but it is a principle that we often forget. Becoming complacent and habitual in our negative behaviors often prevents us from reaching our goals. One of the ways that I would help them get focused on goals was through creating a to-do list of actionable steps that they have control over completing, and they are responsible to nobody but themselves. One of the items on the to-do list was to create a roadmap of their life.

There was no deadline, there was no expectation, and there was no punishment for not completing it. It was simply a way for them to reflect on how specific situations in their past shaped the way they currently behaved, often negative behaviors that hindered their own progress. I would advise them to get a large piece of construction paper and draw an oversized winding road traveling through hills and mountains. Each hill or mountain represented a tough time. If they didn't have access to large construction paper, I would explain how they could tape 6 standard pieces of paper together to have a large enough drawing space. Along the road of their past, I would ask them to create a timeline that lists every significant event in their lives that they feel impacted the way they lived their lives, both positively and negatively. I would encourage them to do a brain dump. Instead of thinking about the details of every situation, I recommended that they simply think about when they had big emotions related to an event, write it down, and then move on. This enabled them to get a "big picture" of where their emotions came from without overthinking and potentially re-living the pain. If someone seemed overwhelmed at the thought of attempting to remember past events, I would simply cross the roadmap off their to-do list and instead help them focus on something they aren't overwhelmed by.

I would sometimes stick around for an hour and help them draw their winding road while discussing better ways to approach triggering situations and how to stay focused on goals. Other times I would help them write down their to-do list and encourage them to start their roadmap as soon as I left. This would give them something to focus on instead of sulking in whatever argument or situation that was recently causing crisis. I wouldn't do this for everyone, but there were specific individuals that I could tell were just ready to have a deeper understanding. When they did this, it was helpful almost immediately. One of my favorite things to discuss with them was their role in "the system." Often times, they would be so disgusted with being stuck in the legal or welfare systems that they would refuse to "play by the rules." This applied to teens in group homes and youth shelters, as well as to drug addicted parents who had their parental rights taken away for child endangerment and exposure to drugs. Helping them focus on their goals and teaching them that "jumping through hoops" was a step towards their goals enabled them to make the decision to improve their behaviors. Again, this was not a requirement in my job, but it improved outcomes and prevented cycles from repeating. In turn, it decreased the amount of calls we may have received for the same person and for the same issue each week. We had many frequent fliers; some of them never seemed to "get it" while others would tell me things like, "After 15 years of going through the system, nobody has ever helped me understand "why" I act this way. I finally get it. Thank you."

I first learned this approach when I was working with the foster youth advisory board in my home state. It was a group activity that the program director would have us facilitate, especially with young people who were new to the organization. The purpose of the roadmap within the youth group was not just to get through a crisis, but to facilitate helping them gain a deeper understanding so that they could help others understand what a foster kid needs. It was one step towards helping them move from being a "victim" to an "advocate;" one who could share his story in a positive way that impacted legislation and educated the community. Later in my career, I found it was very helpful for almost anyone.

Self-reflection can be a powerful thing, but at the same time, it can also be difficult. Being honest with ourselves as we reflect upon the past is part of this difficulty. We have to face our own demons, guilt, and shame while also re-visiting those times when others may have hurt us. Regardless, it is very important to periodically take the time to do so. As this old saying goes, "history repeats itself. But if we take the time to understand our own past, family history, and patterns of behavior, then we no longer leave our futures up to chance. We can take back our own power to create the lives we want. I was reminded of the necessity of self-reflection the hard way when I started writing this book.

CHAPTER 12

TWO ROADMAPS
COMPARED

*"...I still struggled to write down one sentence,
or phrase, at a time that represents a moment
that forever changed my view of the world..."*

Ironically, even with as much as I have helped others with the self-reflection process, it has been a very long time since I had created my own roadmap. Writing this book gave me ample opportunity to reflect upon this, and this chapter specifically was the most difficult, as it contains a timeline of my own past, one that has developed greatly since the last time I drew a long winding road years ago. Some of the chapters in this book have come in one writing session or over the course of one day, while others took several days. But this chapter took several weeks, even months. Not because it took me a long time to write this short introduction paragraph, but because it was extremely difficult to force myself to recall my past and feel comfortable writing it down for the world to see.

It just goes to show how deeply rooted our pains might be no matter our education, career, or experience level. Much like many of the people who may read this book, I have built my career and lifestyle around impacting others and helping people overcome to live happier, healthier, and more successful lives. Yet, I still struggled to write down one sentence, or phrase, at a time that represents a moment that forever changed my view of the world and how I interact within it.

It shows me that if we don't take care of our "crap," it will only pile up and allow us to continue the negative life cycles that prevent us from progressing mentally, emotionally, and even physically. If just one person reads the following moments in my timeline and builds the courage to find a deeper understanding of their behaviors, then I know that this self-exposure was worth the countless hours of pacing in front of my computer screen, building up the courage to write down the happenings that created my own two screens.

When I first started this grueling process, I shared my ideas with a co-worker of mine, Christy. After knowing Christy for only a few short months, she was able to get me to divulge my plans for this book in a way that I would normally never discuss plans or my personal life with a colleague. For some reason, it didn't feel awkward or make me feel exposed. It was like she could see my past through my eyes; the way an attentive mother can see when something is wrong. It was a safe feeling that resembled the unconditional acceptance that I had experienced with only a very few people in my life.

Providing that level of affection comes naturally to Christy, and that makes sense, considering her 30-year therapy career, mostly in juvenile justice. Along the way, she has met many young men, a lot like myself, and my guess is that she has provided that same level of acceptance to every single one of them, even those who have stolen from and lied to her. My guess is they each probably called her from prison to apologize, and she probably still answered the phone every time to tell them that everything will be okay. It takes a special person to fight back with love, and that seems to be exactly what she would do.

One day while we were working together, it was just the two of us hanging out in the office. It was a slow day, so I was working on my book. She started asking more questions about my childhood and I hesitantly answered; most of my other co-workers usually sat in silence working on separate projects during slow times, so her questions were a bit of an adjustment for me. After a lengthy conversation, she said she wanted me to meet someone who reminded her a lot of me. She said he was about my age, and had a very similar childhood as I did, but he had fallen victim to the negative cycles of drugs in his family and was serving yet another prison sentence. His name was Ryan. I nonchalantly agreed to this introduction that would later be carried out through letters that he would mail to her from prison to give to me.

Upon reading the first letter, I noticed some major similarities in the various negative experiences that he and I both shared, so I asked Christy to have him create a timeline. When I received this timeline, it was apparent that Ryan and I had more significant childhood events in common than not. We were even born in the same year.

Recognizing several similarities, all three of us thought that it would be both interesting and beneficial to be able to compare and contrast our two timelines. The below table demonstrates the similarities and differences that influenced each of our decisions, paths, and current lives. In no way do I want this to be a comparison of "good versus bad," because it is very possible that I could have easily ended up in his shoes, and he in mine. That can probably be said for many people, which is why it is so important to never place judgment on others; you never know where they've been or what they're going through.

Christy talked a lot about how intelligent Ryan was, how much potential he had, and how his thoughtfulness and conversations reminded her of my own. According to Christy, he and I were likely have similar intelligence levels. On the other hand, we both made a lot of very poor decisions at young ages. He and I both walked a fine line between living a free life and stepping behind bars. Aside from a couple of nights in a county jail during my college years, I was able to avoid living much of my life in a cell. Regrettably, Ryan wasn't that lucky. Fortunately, it isn't too late, and Ryan has an opportunity to re-build his second screen in which he views the world. While incarcerated, he has been studying psychology through a distance-learning program associated with a nearby community college and plans to transfer to a university upon his release.

My goal for this comparison is to allow a simple visual of the factors that facilitated growth and success for each of us at different stages of life, while also visualizing the barriers that caused each of our paths to veer in the negative direction. I believe that after reviewing our timelines side by side, you will quickly see the similarities in our early childhoods that have perpetuated each of our negative decisions. Along with this, you may notice the differences that may have allowed me to avoid prison, while Ryan has had a bit more of a difficult path to gaining insight and education while reflecting behind bars.

Bolded items = Positive experiences that impacted future emotional wellness and success

Underlined Items = Experiences that are the same, or very similar, for both Travis and Ryan

Similar Trauma, Different Outcomes			
Year	Approx Age	Travis	Ryan
1983	<u>Born</u>	Born, Washington State	Born, California
1986-1989	3-5	<u>Living with mom, dad, and sister</u> near Seattle, WA	<u>Living with mom, dad, and sister,</u> relocated to Virginia Beach, VA Naval Base

Year	Age		
1990	<u>6</u>		Parents separated; mother moved herself, her three daughters, and Ryan to Fremont, NE (near maternal grandparents
1991	7		Parents officially divorced
1992	8	Witnessed domestic violence between parents	<u>First unsupervised experience with liquor.</u>
1993	9	Parents divorced. Dad went to jail for domestic violence. Not able to see Dad. Sister went to drug treatment. Mom stopped working. No longer felt safe. Started displaying negative behaviors and physically fighting with mother.	Began smoking cigarettes in the 5th grade. Was in constant legal trouble; stealing cigarettes, pornography, and fifths of liquor on a regular basis. Twice admitted to a mental health unit for periods of 30 days each (Depression and Pyromania).

1993	9	Mom went to hospital to seek help with mental and emotional health. Travis went to a temporary foster home. Travis went to a temporary foster home. Got picked up by extended family that Travis never knew existed (maternal aunt/ uncle/grandparents) and moved to Iowa from Seattle. Mom and sister moved to Iowa one month later.	Bounced between living with mother and sister and paternal grandparents during 5th and 6th grade. Frequently truant from school and got caught smoking weed. Was given the option of going to Boys Town in Omaha, NE or permanently living with grandparents in Ohio. Chose to live with grandparents. They provided a foundation of moral/social principles before it was "too late,"though they would lay dormant for years.

Year	Age	Events	
1994		Moved in to a trailer with mom and sister Started smoking	
1995	10-13	Got jumped by neighbor kids twice **Started writing love song lyrics** Unhealthy home environment/frequent arguments with mom continued Tried beer for the first time Spent time in a group living facility	Father retired from the US Navy after 18 years of service and moved to Westerville to be near me and his parents. Grandfather receives promotion at work which requires us to move to Broken Arrow, OK.
1996		Spent time in a shelter Spent one month in pediatric mental health unit Joined older kids in stealing out of unlocked cars **Volunteered answering phones at American Red Cross** Switched schools twice	

1997	14	<u>Stealing cigarettes</u> from convenience stores, reselling them to older kids First experience with <u>pornography</u> Sister gave birth to his nephew Saw stripper photo of Mom on pole Friends' older siblings on baseball team saw Mom in club and harassed Travis about it Heard an answering machine recording of his mother saying Travis was a bad kid and in trouble, and that she might as well give me up to state custody	At his request, guardianship is signed over from Ryan's grandparents to his father. He moved to Westerville to live with father and his father's girlfriend.
1998		**Moved in with maternal aunt and uncle - stable home on a farm away from negative influences** Placed on probation for earlier theft crimes	

1998	14	Completed 100 hours community Service **Studied woodworking on farm. Was taught patience and persistence and the importance in having pride in hard work and quality outcomes.** Refinished a crib for nephew. Wanted him to have nice things. **Was forced to pick at least one sport to play during the school year - started wrestling** Quit smoking	Ryan's father gets married. First experiences with court system when Ryan was charged with theft and attempted credit card fraud. He was put through the "Teen Court" system in Columbus, OH.

1999	15	<u>8th grade language arts teacher personally recognized me as "most improved" at the end of the school year</u> Sister overdosed on Meth, almost died. Nephew started bouncing between living with sister, his father and paternal grandmother. Was always worried about him.	Marjorie, Ryan's step mother, commits suicide by prescription medication overdose.
2000	16	Visited Mom most Sundays. She was on over a dozen psychotropic medications and could not function and would rarely remember Travis visiting. **Started a job as a residential counselor taking care of mentally handicapped adults.**	First use of Opium. Began drinking on a constant basis.

2001	17	<u>First relationship.</u> Filled with jealousy, lies and sex. Her father was in prison for drugs. **Started writing poetry**	<u>Met "first love"</u> at concert. This relationship, though immature, would have a profound impact on Ryan's decision making over the next five years. Graduated High School.
2002	18	**Became a Certified Nursing Assistant (CNA) through community college credit offered in high school. His aunt convinced him to follow this career path in order to obtain a higher paying job.** After wrestling season ended, Travis felt a lack of purpose and direction Spent open class periods during senior year drinking beer with a friend Felt bad that he was doing well while his family still had poor lifestyles.	

2002	18	Got involved with a theft ring re-selling stolen electronics. Graduated high school Behaviors worsened again and I got kicked out of my aunt and uncle's home one week after graduation. Became homeless. Snuck into girlfriend's house to sleep. Got a second job and found a cheap apartment with a roommate. Partied all summer while working, but performance at work suffered and nearly lost my jobs. People that my sister used to associate with started coming to my parties. Got in many arguments and one physical fight. **Got sick of living negative lifestyle so I asked my aunt for help. She helped me start college.**	

2002 continued	19	Received first adult legal charge: theft as an accomplice to his girlfriend stealing from a high dollar department store. Moved away to study business at a state university. Joined fraternity Spent weekends visiting girlfriend back home. Tried a sales job, but didn't like it. Started working as a CNA in a nursing home.	Limited information available due to difficulty communicating during Ryan's current running prison sentence during the writing of this book.
2003	19	Nephew moved in with Mom. Sister still struggling with drugs. Switched majors from business to nursing. Arrested for trespassing and simple assault after getting blackout drunk at a frat party. Served 2 days in jail.	

2003	19	Stopped talking to my "first love" Started filling loneliness with casual sex.	Arrested for Armed Robbery. 2-5 years in prison.
2004	20	**Started job as psychiatric technician in mental health unit.** Arrested for DUI (Driving Under the Influence). Served one night in jail and two days of substance abuse class. Still in College. Started spending all his time in an in-home music studio. Developed friendships at the studio and felt accepted. Felt at home there more than he did "going back home".	Residing in prison.

2005	21	In college. Focused on school, work and writing lyrics in the studio. Filled loneliness and boredom with casual sex. Refused to "get close" with anyone.	Paroled to father's house in Westerville, OH
2006	22	Moved to Seattle temporarily to spend time with father during the summer. Worked in trauma centers for a travel agency. Filled boredom and loneliness with casual sex. Rode motorcycle back to Iowa. **Graduated from college with Bachelor's of Science in Nursing (BSN)**	Completed first prison sentence. Arrested for Possession of a Controlled Substance (Klonipin / Clonazepam). Sentenced to 20 months - 5 years in prison.

2007	23	**Got licensed as a Registered Nurse and started job in an emergency department.** **Became regional facilitator of foster youth advisory group in my state.** **Shared his story of Overcoming in public for the first time.** Dated a girl who taught him many lessons about healthy communication. She later left Travis. Casual sex stopped and became abstinent for several months for the first time since he was 16. Relocated to Des Moines, IA to take custody of his nephew and be close to aunt and uncle for support. Started job in pediatric ER.	Paroled to mother's house in Fremont, NE.

2008	24	Sister moved in with nephew and Travis. After 8 months, they moved out on their own. She had finished community college and started a career. Travis received more opportunities to share his story as a public speaker. **Performed his first professionally paid speaking and performing gig in Las Vegas.** Wrote his first ideas for creating a book.	Began injecting opiates and meth.
2009	25	Stopped working with the foster youth council. Studied business with the Small Business Development Center (SBDC).	While on parole, arrested for Check Forgery. 2-4 years in prison.

2009	25	Won a business plan competition for developing a speaking and performance business. Studied the public speaking industry as well as basic web development and online marketing tactics. Built and launched first speaking web site. Refusing to "get close" in any potential romantic relationship.	While on parole, arrested for Check Forgery. 2-4 years in prison.
2010	26	Still working part time in pediatric ER. First time speaking for mental health professionals. Started a side job as a Life Coach with a counseling agency working with teens. Taught life skills and provided in-home support during crisis.	Released ("Jammed Out"), due to overcrowding in the correctional facility, from both concurrently running sentences. Moved back to Fremont, NE.

2010	26	Unsuccessful attempt at growing speaking business to a full time income. Started dating a girl and decided to force myself to "get close".	
2011	27	The girl Travis started dating ended up having more attachment issues than he did. Travis called it off after he realized he had become a built in counselor and she had been dishonest with Travis. He had already become very attached, so this was quite difficult considering the attachments difficulties faced from childhood. Quit working as a Life Coach.	Married Jewel on an overnight whim. Intentional overdose on Depakote / Divalproex Sodium. Stabilized in ER and psychiatric floor at hospital. Released in December.

2011	27	Took a part time job as the school nurse for an alternative high school during 2011-2012 school year. Their original nurse had a child dying from cancer so Travis filled in. This was a very fulfilling experience where he learned a lot about how the education system interacts with other community based services for at-risk youth. Did not speak this year. Was discouraged from failing at growing his business last year.	One week after being released, his wife found Ryan lifeless on the kitchen floor of a friend's apartment after an unintentional overdose while shooting up Fentanyl. Wife performed CPR until medical technicians arrived. Revived and stabilized in ER and psychiatric unit again and released four days later.
2012	28	Started more public speaking again. Struggling to find passion and purpose. Was no longer satisfied in role as a nurse.	Arrested for terroristic threats, assault, and possession of a deadly weapon. 7 years 8 months - 18 years in prison.

2012	28	Started taking pre-requisite science classes with a plan of going to medical school. Still had PRN position with mental health crisis team. Still had part time position as ER nurse. Started as an Adjunct Professor for his alma mater, teaching pediatric clinical rotations for undergraduate nursing students. 1 credit hour per semester. Left position as school nurse.	
2013	29	Cancelled applications to medical school. Was accepted to graduate school to obtain a DNP (Doctoral of Nursing Practice) and become a Psychiatric Nurse Practitioner.	

| 2013 | 29 | Joined a friend in touring to speak and perform for over 10,000 students in collaboration with Gear UP and the Department of Education. Educated and encouraged low income, high risk and minority students to go to college. This re-inspired Travis' passion for speaking and performing.

Spoke several more times this year. Changed ER work status to working as needed/on occasion instead of regular part-time. Started writing his book Overcoming Emotional Trauma.

Made the decision that he did not want to dedicate more years to a career that would require himi to write prescriptions for drugs which he did not believe were always appropriate. Dropped out of the DNP program. | Elected President of Toastmasters Innovators Club at Nebraska State Penitentiary and enrolled in community college through distance learning program. |

2013	29	Changed ER status to PRN (per required needs) Started full time with the crisis team. Still an adjunct professor, 1 credit hour per semester. Started making plans to become self employed as a speaker, author, and consultant.	
2014	30	Launched new web site www.TravisLloyd.net. Started more aggressive marketing, hired personal assistants to assist in business development. Became self employed as an author, speaker, consultant. Still an adjunct professor, 1 credit hour per semester and PRN in ER which allows Travis to maintain licensure as an RN and stay up to date with current practices. **Completed book Overcoming Emotional Trauma.**	Residing at Nebraska State Penitentiary. **Studying psychology with a goal of transferring to a state university upon release.**

"As one can see, even people who share
parallel life experiences may have journeys that
are disparate, and the most obvious reason for
this is probably that each person's experience is
subjective. Two people can have similar, even
identical experiences, and they perceive them
and respond to them in different ways."

~ Dr. Gregory Keck, PhD

CHAPTER 13

SURVIVAL MODE

"You can't always control what events life throws at you, but you can control how you react to them."

I believe that the heightened awareness and racing heart that is often associated with survival mode dates back to less evolved times. It can still be seen to this day in under-developed countries, as well as those plagued by civil wars or terrorism. As I follow the coverage of the people who have had their villages raided and fathers murdered, I notice how survival mode played a role in the aftermath. The photographer, Brandon, from the blog Humans of New York, was asked by the United Nations to partner with them on a world tour in August and September of 2014. Brandon has built his blog by taking a photo of a person and asking them an inquisitive question like, "What was the toughest time of your life?" Some of his photos and statements from Iraq and Uganda show that even after experiencing horrifying deaths or being run out of their villages, the survivors have re-built their settlements, villages, and cities. Using whatever materials they can find, they construct shelters and start growing foods. They also tap in to the electricity set up by the UN using any tin and wire they can find. The need to survive supersedes all other aspects of life.

Families, communities, and villages stay close together in order to depend on each other in time of need. In the time of hunting and gathering, if a person strayed too far from their family, survival mode would kick in. It would give them the energy to be aware of their surroundings and fight, if necessary. Awhile back, I met a man my age who was a refugee from Africa. He told me that he once ran for an entire night to escape from his village that had just been taken over. Survival mode served him well. The goal of this primitive reaction was to stay alive long enough to reunite with his loved ones. After several days of not finding any of his family, he attached to another family unit who then claimed him as his own; his life depended on it.

That may be one of the reasons why many people feel that they need to depend on others. We are hard wired to be with, and support, other people. Attached covers this in great detail, and claims that the term "co-dependency" is an inappropriate term due to the fact that it is natural to depend on others. Hence, the grief felt with the loss of loved one.

As you know, in today's society, it takes a lot less than life threatening situations to be "triggered" into experiencing symptoms of survival mode. I guess this helps makes sense of my past erratic behaviors related to a real, or perceived, relationship loss. My connections to friends, or romantic partners has helped me feel secure and safe, much like it is engraved in our genetic code to do. I would assume that may be why I immediately ask the question, "How will I survive without them?!" Although we can obviously survive without friends, the symptoms of survival mode kick in. The term Survival Mode also has several other potential meanings attached to it.

In the past, I have seen this term used in reference to sales employees who are at risk for losing their job. I once read a Forbes Magazine article titled "5 Signs that Employees are in Survival Mode," which described that such employees become very cutthroat and will do whatever it takes to one-up the next person. Inevitably, that leads to the demise of a sales team, department, or even corporation. I have also seen this term referenced in war-themed video games where the goal of the game is to simply "survive" through any means possible. I imagine that teenage girls whose parents provide them with nearly unlimited credit have even referenced it. Once they run low on funds and are at risk of not being able to have a luxury they are accustomed to, I bet it feels like survival mode. I can also only imagine that their parents feel like they are fighting a war, as well.

If you think about it, the physiologic response is the same: increased heart rate, fear, and panic. Each of those symptoms is present in war, and the teenage girl who might not be able to purchase another $400 of clothes that week may feel this too. It might sound silly, but this reinforces the fact that every person has a different perception as to whether or not an event is seen as traumatic. Regardless, when anyone perceives an event as traumatic, it affects their entire body, mind, spirit, and behaviors. I know this to be true for me, to this day.

You may have noticed in Chapter 9's roadmap that many of both Ryan and my negative behaviors initiated only after experiencing life events that were perceived by society as traumatic. Even when drugs and violence impacted our lives, neither of us ever thought that we were experiencing anything abnormal. Therefore, we were never aware that specific events were traumatic to us. At the time, I would have argued to the grave that I could "handle it" and that it didn't affect me negatively; no matter what it was. I'm sure Ryan would agree. According to both of us, there was a time when we truly believed we were never traumatized.

I believe a lot of people think that way. Since so many people view traumatizing events only as large events, such as a death or serious injury, it makes it easier to not pay attention to the little things. Yet, these little things have such a big impact, even when you might not notice. This goes for us all. My experience as a crisis worker showed me that education, position, and socioeconomic status have no bearing on whether or not someone "could" be traumatized. Often times, survival mode behaviors, caused as a result of traumatizing experiences, would go unrecognized by the individual I was serving.

While writing this chapter, I met a woman who had previously seen some of my videos and magazine articles online. The reason we met was that she was struggling to be happy and develop social relationships due to several insecurities. She wanted advice for overcoming these feelings. Her first statement to me was that she didn't think she had anything to overcome, and that she has "just always been that way," as she, "never had anything bad happen, like going to foster care." She said that she felt very blessed knowing that she had the "perfect life" and had "never been traumatized."

As we began talking, it was apparent that she was experiencing survival mode on a regular basis. She struggled to make her own decisions and was deathly afraid of conflict. Anytime she would face an argument, she would completely forget what she was mad about and never re-visit the issue. Not just a proverbial "I forgot," but actually no longer recalling the conversation. It was as if she completely blacked out. She wished very badly that she could begin to understand how to do basic things like add windshield washer fluid to her car, or understand what the cruise control icon represented when the light came on.

I found all of this very intriguing, considering her profession. She happened to be a resident physician in charge of the care of dozens of hospitalized patients every day. Yet, she couldn't handle personal relationships or arguments without mentally "checking out," which is her sign of survival mode. In order to help her gain a deeper understanding of these behaviors, it was important to peel back the layers of traumatizing experiences. When did this start? Why did it start? Was there anything specific triggering this behavior or did numerous tiny stressors add up over time? Are you happy? Why not?

There may be defense mechanisms that cause traumatized individuals to avoid answering questions directly, or by giving only partial answers. This helps avoid facing the deeper level of pain. I did that when I was younger by completely forgetting any negative experiences; they later came back as bad dreams. This young woman did so prior to me ever asking "Why?" This defensiveness was demonstrated by initially stating that she felt she had a "perfect upbringing." Minimizing the impact of potential traumatizing experiences is a battle that we all fight. As a friend, professional, or family member who cares, this makes tracing the cause of survival mode slightly more complicated. This can easily bring you off track from identifying the "root" problem in a crisis situation or personal relationship. Minimizing your own experiences can do the same thing for your emotional development. There is more to asking "Why?" than simply asking "Why?"

Critical Thinking Moment: Have you allowed someone's avoidance to take you off track from gaining a deeper understanding of your personal or professional relationship with them? Are there things in your life that you avoid answering when someone brings up a touchy subject? It is important to ask yourself whether avoiding those touchy subjects is a healthy way to cope, or if it feeds in to behaviors that inhibit your personal growth.

The root cause of her being "triggered" into survival mode was easy to trace. She talked highly about having everything she needed as a child, but when I asked about how often she talks with her parents, her tone changed. She stuttered and brushed it off saying, "We just don't talk very often." After opening that can of worms, she fearfully exposed her discontent with having controlling parents and minimized it as being "a part of Asian culture." She is Korean.

Until this point, she had never put two and two together. She had successfully avoided understanding her behaviors by throwing herself into school. Upon completing medical school, the 12-hour night shifts for six days each week as a resident physician, served her avoidance quite well. Her insecurities, fear of trying new things, and difficulty making decisions were a direct result of her "perfect" childhood. Her childhood consisted of very few hugs and little recognition for her high scholarly achievements. It was always met with, "I expected better from you." No matter how much society may normalize such experiences, the symptoms of survival mode that show through blocking memories of stressful arguments don't develop spontaneously. Not being allowed freedom to make her own decisions or be validated through positive praise was the obvious "root cause" of her symptoms/behaviors.

When not preserving life, survival mode can easily be seen as a bad thing. This is true, to a certain extent, considering it is definitely not a good thing to enter survival mode in professional settings or when dealing with sensitive interpersonal (close) relationships. However, for this young physician - and other people of all backgrounds - survival mode is a necessary aspect of self-preservation. If our minds don't block out feelings associated with past traumatic experiences, we run the risk of allowing our emotions to go right back to an initial traumatizing experience. In turn, this would impair our ability to function at our highest possible level. But what can we do to get out of survival mode? How do you even start when everything in life seems so difficult right now? Here are some initial steps you can take and should keep in mind if you ever find yourself falling into survival mode again:

Finding the Root of the Problem

I mentioned before that unless you identify what the root of what is triggering your survival mode is, you're only applying a Band-Aid solution by treating the symptoms and not the cause. Finding the root of what has caused your survival mode may not be easy. It may be an ongoing process instead of something you can identify in a day. You will likely need the help of a counsellor or friend to talk through what you is bothering you and what underlying issues might be causing that distress. Don't be afraid to accept advice and guidance. An outside perspective is of utmost importance.

Many things that affect you in your adult life link back to your childhood, whether they be good or bad things. Think back to your childhood, starting with a general overview. Do you think you had a healthy childhood? Were your parents or guardians nurturing and affectionate or controlling and critical? Was there financial stability or did your parents struggle paycheck to paycheck? Next, think about some major events or milestones of your childhood e.g. moving, getting awards, getting a sibling. Finally, think of the specific memories that pop into your head when you imagine your childhood. What are those memories and why do they stand out so much for you? These little memories can sometimes be the most crucial for identifying what issues may have arisen in your childhood that affects your behavior today.

Think of the major traumatic experiences in your life. Did those get addressed after they happened or did you suppress the event and try to "keep calm and carry on?" Bottling things up can only be an effective tactic for so long. If those events have not been addressed, this may be the cause of your present survival mode. Even if you did seek therapy or counseling after something happened to you, you may not have fully completed the healing process. The counselors and therapists cannot "fix" you. It is imperative to develop and consistently maintain a lifestyle of personal development and make sure your psyche has resolved any issues surrounding those events.

Substance use is simultaneously a great clue to what is causing our survival mode and is also one of the factors that can cause the most confusion. The same can be said for the dangerous use of casual sex, as I have mentioned throughout the book. Some people mistake drug or alcohol addiction as their sole issue, while the addiction is actually masking underlying issues. My friend Anthony (name changed) has a father, Peter, with a history of severe alcohol abuse. Peter was often physically and verbally abusive with Anthony, becoming angry when he drinks. If left to his own devices, he would eat very poorly, his apartment would become a mess, and his finances would dwindle from spending it all on alcohol and fast food. He had gone to rehab three times, and each time he got out, he would begin drinking again, almost immediately. Eventually, a doctor identified him as schizophrenic and began him on a treatment of an antipsychotic and an antidepressant. Since being on the medication, he has not had a drink or even felt like drinking, and is getting his life back together. This is just one example of someone living in survival mode who had not found the root of the problem. His alcohol abuse was self-medicating the suffering and anxiety he felt as a result of his mental illness. In reference to the use of medications, I would like to share that I have personally met someone who has fully recovered from a schizophrenia diagnosis. Although very rare, especially in America, such recovery is possible, not for everyone, but some. Using psychotropic medications can be a very useful tool, but eventually could also be the culprit of masking root causes. Although you may not be abusing street drugs, prescription drugs or alcohol, but using it occasionally, ask yourself what triggers you craving a cigarette or a drink. Is it when you remember a bad relationship, or after a supervisor speaks harshly to you at work? Finding out what makes you crave certain things can be a good indicator of the excessive stress causing your survival mode.

Make a Big-Picture Plan

Just as it is important to recognize the root of the problem, instead of only seeing the superficial issues, you need to make a plan to rebuild a strong foundation to your life rather than only trying to fix the symptoms. It would be like trying to build a brick house on sand. Sure, the house may stand up against the elements, but the faulty groundwork will eventually give out.

Finding time for yourself is important for getting out of survival mode. I understand that between work, children, volunteering, and whatever else you might have on your plate, this can seem like a daunting task, but try to find little ways to affirm your self-worth and prevent yourself from becoming burnt out. Consider trying meditation. It doesn't have to be a spiritual thing if you don't want it to be, and even five minutes of keeping your mind clear, being present in your body, and breathing deeply can make you feel amazing! Read a couple pages of a book or comic before bed. It doesn't take that long to read three pages, and doing so will make you feel like you've relaxed at least a little (plus you can distract yourself from your worries with the story you're reading).

Related to finding time for yourself is staying organized. For me, I often struggle to write or focus on projects with deadlines until I have organized my living space and created a to-do list. The more organized you are, the more you will find opportunities to take a few minutes to relax. Pack lunches for the children or your spouse the night before so you aren't rushing around. Make a list of things to do each day or get a day planner. One of my newly acquired organizational habits is writing a list of the three most important items/projects that I have to complete for the day. Below each project, I list three to five to-do items that will help get each project done. I prioritize the projects in order of importance and start with the most important first, completely ignoring the other projects and to-do items until the first is complete. Having an organized schedule might not solve your relationship or financial troubles, but it will help in developing a strategy to get out of survival mode and begin living life fully present again.

Open Up

I cannot impress upon you enough the importance of reaching out to others. Venting about what stresses you out or sharing a traumatic experience is essential to the healing process because it makes you feel recognized. Humans want visibility and recognition by others; when another person acknowledges us, it helps solidify a sense of identity. We recognize the "I" by realizing what is "not I." Stress and trauma erode a person's sense of identity, self-worth, and subjectivity. In a scenario like sexual assault, this is more obvious to see: the attacker has made the survivor feel like an object by violating their body. But sometimes, being made to feel like an object can be through little things that happen every day, being ignored or talked down to be a boss or loved one or living for others instead of taking time for yourself. Sharing your experiences with a trusted individual can help to rebuild yourself and rescue you from survival mode.

Many people hold things inside them because they feel like they would be "weak" if they seek outside help, or maybe they feel guilty or like a bother because, "my problem isn't that bad, other people have lives that are way worse." No person is self-sufficient, so seeking help from others is an inevitable and necessary part of life. Even when I was the one talking a suicidal man off the bridge, I still sought help to maintain my emotional wellness. Swallow your pride; you're hurting yourself and potentially others in your life by staying in survival mode out of stubbornness. Feeling guilty or like you are a bother is also something you shouldn't worry about. As I mentioned before, everyone experiences stress differently. What might not be upsetting for one person might traumatize another; trauma is in the eye of the beholder. Try to forgive yourself for having a unique reaction to an event or events.

If you really feel uncomfortable reaching out to a therapist or friend, or you don't think you have a support group you can really trust, try writing down your thoughts and experiences. The "roadmap" exercise mentioned in chapter 9 is a great structure to utilize if you are truly ready to tackle your past. Writing a blog or a journal entry is helpful with immediate needs. Suzette Henke writes in her book Shattered Subjects that "scriptotherapy," or writing down your traumatic experiences, can still help you make sense of what has happened to you and make you feel heard, even if you don't ever show someone what you've written down. What matters more is that you release what you're holding inside. Only then can you start on the road out of survival mode.

Don't get caught in a loop

Groundhog Day was a great movie, but living through the same day, repeating the same patterns over and over again can be unproductive and unhealthy, especially when they are causing you stress or re-traumatizing you. Many people gravitate towards structure and stability and our mind likes to get into habits. Making sure you have healthy habits rather than ones that keep you unhappy and from accomplishing the goals you want in life is key.

Have you ever had a song stuck in your head? Pretty annoying, right? Sometimes I have trouble sleeping because I have a song stuck in my head that just won't go away. The reason we get songs stuck in our head is because our minds get trapped in a loop. Usually you repeat the same section of the song continuously until you listen to the song again. If you aren't able to listen to the song at the moment, a good tactic for getting that pesky music out of your head is by imagining what the end of the song sounds like.

Your brain recognizes the song as finished and you can lay that dog to rest. What does this have to do with survival mode? Well, just like you can get a song stuck in your head, you can fall into anxiety loops that cause excessive worry.

Whether you have an anxiety disorder or not, I'm sure at some point in your life you've experienced an anxiety loop, where you keep running a scenario over in your head again and again, wondering what went wrong, what you could have done differently. These loops can happen even with things that haven't happened yet! You worry about future scenarios, how they could go, what you should do, if you'll be good enough to rise to whatever challenge you might face. These loops can be incessant and cause you to sweat, your heart to race, maybe you even have a panic attack. In a similar way to getting a song out of your head, you need to put that loop to rest to save yourself further (and usually unnecessary) stress.

One of the causes of stress is your mind recognizing a task as incomplete. That's one of the reasons anxiety loops can become so unrelenting; you are probably remembering a scenario wrong, or if you are thinking about a future matter, there is no possible way to figure out the outcome because it hasn't happened yet. If you are remembering a past event and it keeps coming back to haunt you, the reason you can't find a solution to the problem is because the problem you are imagining may not exist. Really reflect on what you are worrying about and ask yourself if you're making a bigger deal out of the scenario than it really warrants. If you're worrying about a future scenario, stop it! You have absolutely no control over something you haven't even been faced with yet; to worry about it is futile. You can't always control what events life throws at you, but you can control how you react to them.

If you find yourself brooding excessively, find ways to distract yourself. Exercise, especially something like yoga or Pilates, which focuses on the mind-body connection and concentrating on your breathing, is great because it forces you to focus on your breath, rather than whatever it is you were worrying about. You could also go for a walk, read a book or magazine, or even clean your house. Whatever you have to do to make sure your time spent turning things over in your mind doesn't prevent you from actually living your life.

Critical Thinking Moment: Just as every person has a different personality, stress can appear in unique ways. You may look at a list of signs and symptoms of stress and find that not all of it (or maybe even none of it) applies to you. When you have time to reflect, write down what nervous habits you have or what seems to happen physically when you are stressed. Knowing how you personally manifest symptoms of survival mode can help in maintenance and prevention of survival mode.

CHAPTER 14

JABS-TO-THE-SIDE

"...good intentions paired with a lack of consideration for where somebody comes from, what they've been through, or what their hopes and dreams are is no better than looking them in the face, smiling brightly, and telling them they will never be as good as someone else."

As a child living through traumatic experiences and mental and emotional anguish, I often found myself getting in trouble and doing things that were out of character. I lacked stability, unconditional love, and guidance, and felt powerless as a result. Quite simply, I had a void in my life. In order to fill this void, I broke rules, attempted to belittle others in hopes of feeling superior, and eventually broke laws for the first time by the ripe age of 11. In my powerless world, negative attention offered a sense of power. I subconsciously chose to get in trouble, and at a young age, I fully accepted and mentally prepared myself for consequences as severe as potential prison time.

Still, deep down inside there was a glimmer of kindness, hope, and innocence that occasionally crept through during these younger years. It would be demonstrated through random acts of kindness such as smiling and holding a door, or offering to help when observing someone struggling. To this day, I still feel at my best when serving others. However, at that time of living life through the eyes of survival mode my natural desire to help others remained suppressed by anger, hatred, and discontent. This brings up a valid point: that we as humans are born with an innate ability to love and serve others. Our experiences train us to adopt negative and hurtful behaviors as a result of self-preservation. When it is not to preserve life, it is to preserve our ego, feelings, or perceived sense of self. As you might guess by the title of this book, the negative aspect often resulted from constantly feeling unsure of life and angry about the cards I had been dealt. My negative "screen" would even consider ways to make things more difficult for others, strictly out of spite.

Occasionally, the brighter side of me received positive affirmation as a result of adults, or peers who I looked up to, observing the kinder behaviors. This came through the form of verbal recognition. It often sounded like, "Wow, I didn't know you had it in you!" or simply, "Thank you, that was very thoughtful of you." Receiving a genuine smile and eye contact reinforced these statements significantly and helped me see that the people behind those statements were much more emotionally mature than me. I had mixed feelings about this, though. On one hand, I was appreciative, while on the other I was irritated that it blatantly highlighted my downfalls and lack of emotional intelligence. It has been said that awareness is key. Yet, for many years, this awareness did nothing until it was paired with an expanded knowledge base, a burning desire for personal development, and individuals who showed me there was a better way to live that did not include a constant state of reactivity or anxiousness.

This positive reinforcement was one of the things that eventually allowed me to begin the life-long journey of overcoming my past, accepting myself for who I believe I am, and simply being happier. I read a line once that stated, "Your value can be found in how others view you." While one might argue that we should find value in ourselves, there is truly something to be said for the fact that how others view you has a direct correlation to how you view yourself. I would venture to say that for an emotionally fragile individual who still struggles with overcoming the past, such as I once was, these external affirmations can make or break one's capacity to successfully overcome even the smallest real or perceived barrier in one's life. This is why I feel it is important for us to have a greatly expanded self-awareness of even the slightest negative experience that creates the lens with which we view our individual worlds and those around us. No matter your job title or social or economic status, it is inevitable that the slightest negative experience, or even the misperception of an experience, can and will create a wealth of prejudices and judgments. If not actively seeking awareness of these pre-conceived notions, these prejudices eventually slip through the fingers of kind-intentions and show themselves as slight jabs to the side.

Balancing both of my screens was a difficult task, as it is for many. My self-esteem and negative behaviors reflected the chaotic maneuvering of a less than ideal life. Meanwhile, the naturally kind and innocent person I once was, and later found again, occasionally shined through. You can imagine the confusion it might cause someone who observed both personas. This is especially true if they personally had not experienced similar chaos. I'm sure that watching me transition from negative screen to positive screen was a shock to some people. Therefore, the positive statements that lifted me up often ended with a slight jab to the side in the form of statements like, "Wow, thank you. Good job! It's about time; you should try that more often." Although likely well intended, it was very crippling to me. They might as well have said, "Good job on that one, but you still suck at life and you'll never get better." You could say the same for the statement mentioned earlier, "Wow! I didn't know you had it in you!" That's how it felt to me and I can imagine it would feel the same to you.

Critical Thinking Moment: Have you ever had someone talk down to you with slight jabs to the side? Have you ever been the one talking down to someone else? Maybe you didn't mean to, but that is how it came out. Some people can handle it and some people are very hurt by it. If you catch yourself giving a proverbial jab to someone's side, don't hesitate to apologize. If you have even an ounce of empathy, apologizing will help relieve the guilt from watching the person you talked down to experience the related emotional pain. Likewise, if it is happening to you and it makes you feel bad, don't be afraid to let them know in a kind way that does not instigate an argument. Simply stating what you want and how you expect to be treated in the future can go a long way.

I would like to offer a very practical example of stating what you want. When I first started working in an emergency department, I worked with a woman who had a very motherly presence. She was generally very kind, but occasionally very brash and firm - as most mothers can be at times. The only issue was that I was not her child, yet her motherly instinct remained and occasionally showed itself through a smack to my head or a flick of the finger to my neck. I went along with it at first because I enjoyed feeling mothered; something I lacked for many years. But after a while, such instances occurred less out of playfulness and more out of reprimand. It was often paired with statements that challenged my professional ability and competency. It began to feel very belittling. At that point, the head smacks and finger flicks triggered me to feel very defensive, as I once did in difficult situations as a child. I tried saying, "Please don't" a few times, but she brushed it off. To her, it was still interpreted as just playing around. But to me it became hurtful. It finally improved once I clearly stated what I expected from our relationship as co-workers. The next time I got a smack to the head, I looked her in the eyes and with a serious tone stated, "Please do not ever touch me again. I don't like it and do not feel that it is appropriate." It caught her off guard and she seemed offended, but she got over it. I never had to deal with feeling belittled again and she began treating me as a colleague rather than as her child. Eventually, we became friendly again.

I have observed these types of jabs to the side in many settings. As noted earlier in the book, during my previous careers I spent time as a registered nurse and mental health professional. My working environments ranged from inpatient psychiatric units to life coaching and community based mental health crisis intervention, among others including the above example from a hospital emergency department. It was inevitable that I would encounter vulnerable populations in every one of these roles. When I first began working in health care, I observed jabs-to-the-side to vulnerable individuals, but accepted it as part of the job. As I grew personally, gradually gaining wisdom and experience, I realized that these jabs were often likely due to the professional simply not taking a holistic viewpoint of their client's case or current situation. Maybe not intentionally, but all too often the lenses that they viewed their work through were skewed with their own judgments and misperceptions. This was likely the result of their own traumatic experiences related to previous work, relationships, or more common childhood issues.

Here is an example of a jab to the side: if a staff member's job was to support a client in daily activities, he might instead do everything for the client without giving the client a chance to expand their ability. If the client were to attempt to do more for themselves, the staff member might shut down their attempts by making statements such as, "You know you can't do that" or "shouldn't do that." A more extreme example would be that same staff member making commanding statements such as "Don't touch that!" or "You're always in my way when I'm trying to help you!"

In turn, the client's progress towards personal achievement goals would be abruptly halted by a glass ceiling created by those jabs that likely stemmed from good intentions. However, good intentions paired with a lack of consideration for where somebody comes from, what they've been through, or what their hopes and dreams are is no better than looking them in the face, smiling brightly, and telling them they will never be as good as someone else.

Through my various roles, I was often nearby when such injustices occurred between professional staff members and clients. I am not intending to mock such professionals, as I have been at fault myself and recognize that it is human nature to respond to stressful situations in a way that protects one's ego. Some people understand this sooner than others, while some may never get it, not for lack of ability, but mostly for a lack of willingness to exercise empathy. Once I "got" it, I felt horrible every time I observed such injustice. It often reminded me of when I felt powerless as a child losing every bit of normalcy I once knew. I found that most of the time these issues came about as a result of one of several things: a lack of knowledge of a specific issue that is important to the other person, a lack of willingness to exercise empathy, or a power trip by the individual. It was often made worse by the individual being fed up and burnt out.

After a while, I gained the courage to stop observing these jabs-to-the-side and start stepping in. Doing so allowed me to be involved in a solution-focused manner without being emotionally entangled. I recognized that every person's voice matters. Not just mine or the individual on the receiving end of the well-intended, or not well-intended jab-to-the-side, but also the person on the delivering end. Both of these often had a point to prove, emotional needs to be met, and certain expectations. Facilitating meeting the needs of both sides without causing the situations to escalate isn't easy and sometimes it requires knowing when it is time to step out; you don't always have to save the day. When things are out of your control, sometimes it is better to let bad things happen and get as far away as possible. Yet if you feel comfortable doing so, making a good-hearted attempt is always worth it.

It might be surprising to you, the wide array of professionals who engaged in such situations; many of whom the general public might least expect due to their position or education. Sometimes it was a nurse in a psych unit. Sometimes it was a police officer. Sometimes it was a principal or teacher. Sometimes it was a director or supervisor of a youth group home for those living with chronic mental illness. Still, other times it was direct care staff barely making a significant enough hourly wage to care whether or not they paid attention to the kids whose lives revolved around an unforgiving disciplinary point system in an understaffed youth shelter or group home. It wasn't always my place or my role, but I just could not walk away when I knew there was an opportunity to make a positive impact in a stressful situation. I have found that when we do things for the right reason with good intentions in a caring manner, positive things tend to happen. Things might not always go as you planned, but offering encouragement and insight to both sides, more often than not, helps everyone feel better. Remembering this and actively seeking opportunities to help someone work through a stressful time has helped me fulfill my desire to serve others.

You might not have a career that places you in constantly stressful situations such as dealing with suicide threats or potentially physically violent behaviors. However, there are still many opportunities to lend an ear or offer a helpful comment in any personal or professional relationship. All it takes is being the one who steps up when everybody else turns a blind eye to the bully who talks down to someone who doesn't have the courage to fight for themselves.

Critical Thinking Moment: Have you ever passed up an opportunity to stop someone from belittling a friend, family member, coworker, or client? What would it take for you to stand up for "the underdog" in the future?

Simply saying, "it's not my problem" is a copout. We all have a responsibility to help and ensure that every person around us feels safe and secure. Doing this for others not only helps them overcome, but also boosts your confidence in your own ability. A boost of confidence is sometimes the missing ingredient in taking one more step towards your own overcoming and reaching, or enhancing, self-actualization.

When it comes to dealing with the many jabs to the side that we will receive in our lives, it is important to remember that when you are on the receiving end, it is never your fault. Yes, there may be times when you mess up or do something inappropriate, but nobody has the right to diminish your self-worth through belittling statements. Speak up for yourself, even when it may be outside of your comfort zone to do so normally. And if you witness jabs to the side happening to others, don't be afraid to stand up for them. There is power in numbers, and no bully can stand up to a large group of people. Having the courage to fight back with wit and kindness may even help that bully become more aware of how their behaviors negatively impact others.

CHAPTER 15

AWARENESS IS KEY

"I finally accepted that my failed relationships were a result of my own behaviors."

I learned the hard way that asking "why" doesn't only apply to seeking a deeper understanding of others who appear to be displaying "crazy" behaviors like being selfishly manipulative, demanding, chaotic, or disruptive. Instead, it applies to you and me, the ones who might be observing the crazy. When you are surrounded by enough "crazy," you tend to normalize abnormal behaviors. From the relative who always gets angry when discussing certain topics and refuses to engage in civil conversation, to the person at work who has to have things a certain way or they will use their political power to get you fired; adapting to and accepting such behaviors causes you to become numb to them. There is also the potential for beginning to mindlessly engage in the same negative behaviors. Some of the "crazy" behaviors are unavoidable and you have no choice but to adapt. But most of the time, making the difficult decision to not spend large amounts of time around your manipulative relative or to find a new job is one way to have control over the behaviors that you are exposed to. Working to avoid them helps prevent you from becoming numb to them and replicating the negative cycle. Becoming numb to even the slightest hint of "crazy" makes it very easy to start to see abnormal things as very normal parts of everyday lives. In turn, it also becomes easy to overlook our own current negative behaviors that have been induced by current or past stressful situations and inevitably impacts our ability to live healthier, happier, and more successful lives. To be sure, I am no stranger to becoming numb and normalizing abnormal behaviors, myself.

Building my career as a motivational speaker gave me a skewed perception of my current life during any given year in my 20's. You see, I built my presentations on the platform of "overcoming" and being successful. I had an "Against All Odds" image of myself, when most people who have faced similar odds are dead, in jail, or even worse, living unsuccessful mediocre and poverty-stricken lives. To reinforce some of these odds, please allow me to share one simple, yet very powerful fact. A report released by Casey Family Programs in 2011 states that a range of 3 to 11 percent of alumni from the foster care system have graduated with a bachelor's degree by the age of twenty-five (1). That's a pretty harsh reality to face when the general population graduates university at a rate closer to 28 to 50 percent.

Fighting these types of odds does something to a person's approach to life. As you may have heard, people who face extreme difficulties are often more ambitious and focused, and less likely to be driven off track from significant accomplishments or goals. This includes the willingness to go without sleep, take on huge undertakings, and do what many others are not willing to do; even at the expense of healthy relationships and other things that most people find value in. You have to be very numb to many things to pull this off.

I've noticed that nearly every movie I see which depicts a CIA agent who is "trained to kill" usually targets having the main character be a "hard" kid who grew up in an orphanage; the characters seem to have nothing to lose. Everything that usually matters to a human does not exist in their lives; unconditional love, family, attachments to people or places, it just isn't there. These movie characters appear to be the perfect machine. This is also the same reason why pimps and human traffickers target girls who live in group homes, an issue that has been reported in all 50 U.S. states. I haven't read it myself (and I'm not sure that I would admit it if I did), but I have heard that the ever-so-popular 50 Shades Of Gray also depicts the extremely driven and successful main character as coming from a detached traumatized childhood.

In no way would I compare myself to any of the above extreme examples, but I feel like I can relate. Having graduated from university at the age of 23, establishing two stable careers during my 20's, achieving a childhood dream of being paid to be on stage, writing a book, becoming a Google certified contributing author in a magazine, and avoiding prison, I feel that I successfully beat the odds originally set against me as a child spending more than 30 days in foster care before the age of 13. In case you are not familiar, "Google certified" simply means that an online magazine that is certified to provide news sources to Google authorities has vouched for my contributions. Being Google certified improves the search engine ranking of articles that are written by a certified author.

When I discuss my schedule with some people, they often become exhausted just hearing about my daily routines of networking, writing, contract preparation, traveling, managing renters in the spare rooms of my home, managing virtual assistants and web developers, exercising, and so forth. To most, it seems not possible. For the life of me, I can't count the amount of times I have run into people who do not believe me when I share about my interests, travels, experiences, and lifestyle of happiness. Sadly, most people I run into seem afraid of doing what would make them happy as they have become numb to complacency and physically and emotionally unhealthy habits. Some of them find happiness and success in the relationships they hold with their family. Others share similar ambition and drive and are willing to "do whatever it takes." Usually they have a pretty intense life story that drives their hunger for knowledge, wisdom and success; much the same as Mr. Gray and I. Unfortunately, also like Mr. Gray, I managed to make it through my 20's without building a healthy romantic relationship.

I am definitely not a millionaire corporate executive like Mr. Gray, and my youth rap-sheet would never allow me aboard the CIA train, but there have been more people than I can count who have offered praise related to my successes, calling me "a miracle" due to the odds I faced as a youth. The fact that 70% of youth who age out of the foster care system end up in prison might have something to do with that. I didn't believe it the first time I heard someone reference me as "a miracle," but after hearing it dozens of times in half-a-dozen states from people who know me well, along with complete strangers, I started to re-think it. And after remembering the state of mind that once allowed me to be completely accepting of the fact that my lifestyle at the age of 18 or 19 might put me in prison for 25 years, I accepted it as a miracle as well.

The week before I turned 20, I got a tattoo across my upper back to remind me of what I overcame. This tattoo reads "Against All Odds." Ironically, this was during a six month period when both my sister and mother were going through very significant life struggles, and I had just been to jail for the second time; fortunately, it became the last time ever. I may have stolen the phrase used for my tattoo from a 2pac song title that was on his rap album that played on repeat for an entire 12 months at the age of 19, but it stood true for me then and still does today. Every time someone asks about it and every time I catch a glance of it in the bathroom mirror, it reminds me of the times when I was so complacent and numb to "crazy" that I was willing to accept the decision to face a life of prison as fate.

Now that I am older, I sometimes wish that my back was not blemished with ink, but I am thankful for the continued reminder. This tattoo reminds me that I am still at risk of becoming numb to abnormal behaviors; especially when I attempt to find my value in my successes, which is another side effect of "doing what it takes". Doing what it takes often includes avoiding the difficult task of self-reflection to identify whether or not we have become numb to self-destructing behaviors and accepting them as a normal part of everyday life. It prevents us from recognizing that something that may appear "normal" is actually a very abnormal situation. Repeated abnormal situations or one large significant situation have the ability to cause trauma in our lives which impacts how we interact in relationships at work and home.

Many people hear the term "trauma" and don't feel it applies to them. However, as a nurse and mental health crisis worker, I have observed that many unhappy relationships, lives, and careers stem from some sort of traumatizing experience that prevents us from living a happier, healthier, and more satisfying life. It is important to remember that trauma is defined by the person living it, not by someone dictating whether it qualifies as "trauma" or not. Experiences as simple as not receiving the Christmas gifts you always asked for as a child may seem insignificant as an adult, but could truly have long-term negative effects on one's life and happiness. I encourage you to reflect on any situation in your past that has prevented you from having better outcomes in any aspect of life. Opening your heart and mind to take an inventory of any and all emotional issues that may inhibit your sense of self-worth or confidence can be a scary thing. Even people in high paying jobs may have several emotionally traumatic issues that cause specific downfalls they wish to overcome. These issues may show themselves in major ways, such as having a life devastated by drugs, or in more subtle ways such as constantly being irritated by things one cannot control. Some people are aware of their issues while some are completely oblivious to how others view their interactions. Either that or they refuse to acknowledge it. I can't always blame them, really. It is tough to face your demons and go out of your comfort zone. For me, it has been a long and uncomfortable road; but once I found the strength to do this uncomfortable work, it was well worth it and I believe it can be for you as well.

As you may well know, being aware of your own trauma and how it affects you in the present moment is a great way to be in charge of your own life, actions, and success (or lack of success). I often call awareness a pre-requisite to "making life happen" instead of "letting life happen to you." In my own life, I found that it is important to make a conscious effort to recognize when my anxiety or negative behaviors are driven from an emotional reaction. Recognizing that my reaction, or over-reaction, may be related to a past event helps me gain awareness of my trauma. Being consistent in analyzing my own behaviors and responses was the key to being able to point out what behavior patterns in my younger years caused me to act or react negatively in the current moment. Sometimes I have been able to identify exact instances in my past, while other times I've simply been able to identify only how I felt in past experiences. Sometimes behaviors are based upon habit, while others may be long-forgotten habits that come back during stressful times. Either way, recognizing that a negative behavior doesn't feel good is a simple tool that allows you to be aware of negative patterns. The associated negative feelings allow you to be aware that you do not want to continue repeating the behaviors that cause the feelings.

It has taken me my entire life to identify past traumas and recognize how they still impact my interactions with others. There is no doubt in my mind that doing the hard work of becoming self-aware was the first step towards living a much happier life. It was also the first step in recognizing that my past does not define me. A quote that I repeat time and time again when supporting individuals who find their identity in a mental health diagnosis is, "Your experiences are not who you are."

Critical Thinking Moment: Can you identify a few of the hills and mountains in your own road map that have potentially impacted your current view of life, relationships and happiness? What situations that still happen today cause you to feel the same negative feelings (i.e. sad, frustrated, worried, anxious) that you did when you had the initial potentially traumatizing experiences? These situations are your "triggers." Being aware of and acknowledging that your triggers exist will put you on your path to being happier, healthier, and more successful - in however you define success. Overcoming them is possible.

Keep in mind that trauma is in the eye of the beholder. Do not allow social stigma or the fear of being judged cause you to minimize experiences that left an impression on one of your actively running screens. It is also important to note that even those who have been on a successful path of overcoming may still have behaviors that they are unaware of. I've been there, and you could be, too. Admitting this fact is not a sign of weakness, but rather is an additional weight lifted off your shoulders. It's a great feeling.

Although certain experiences may have shaped your current behaviors, being aware of them is what can give you the strength to make a conscious decision to change them. We each have the power to create our life. This may sound like a simple concept; but for someone who has never been able to "let it go," it is the battle of a lifetime. For a long time, I struggled to let things go that bothered me to the point of fixation, which prevented me from making progress. Not everyone who is impacted by past experiences has large obvious signs like fixation. Sometimes it is much more subtle, such as avoiding confrontation, the inability to try new things, or being so afraid of failure that you never try for the very thing that could bring you joy. One of my favorite old sayings related to this topic is, "The secret to success is getting started" - Author Unknown.

For me, there came a time when the pain of not addressing my past stressors, or traumas, became worse than the fear of confronting them and taking a risk of losing everything to gain happiness. When I reached this point, I had to make the crucial decision to change or remain the same. After several years of living repeated negative life cycles of unhealthy romantic relationships, avoiding interaction with family members, and neglecting my own emotional health, I finally accepted that my failed relationships were a result of my own behaviors. Even though the behaviors were initiated by past traumatic experiences, reaching that level of awareness placed the responsibility in my own hands to overcome them and helped me stop making excuses or blaming others. It took me until I hit the age of 30 when I saw the joy that my old college buddies had in building a family that I realized how important that type of unconditional love and attachment truly is for me; this despite the fact that I spent my entire life avoiding them and seeking higher levels of personal success.

It has also helped me adjust my focus from finding my value in my personal success to finding it in how well I am able to build and maintain healthy friendships and relationships. I realized that my personal success is much more enjoyable when I get to share it with people who truly care about me and not just my accomplishments. I still have a lifestyle that most would call "crazy" due to how many things I am involved in and projects that I take on; yet being aware allows me to recognize when I might want to use those projects as an escape. Recognizing this allows me to make a conscious decision to not utilize my busy lifestyle to avoid life, but instead help me to re-focus my energy on what is truly important in life: people and relationships.

CHAPTER 16

TAKING ACTION

"...this lifestyle can be learned and implemented at any time by anyone who is willing to push themselves mentally, emotionally and yes, even physically."

The first time I ever spoke in public I was shaking. I was supposed to share my story about facing adversities while growing up in foster care to a group of lawyers. There was no specific structure; I was simply told, "Tell your story." So, I did. I thought I did a horrible job and could not see the purpose of such self-exposure due to my own negative self-talk. Still, afterwards, I received great reviews and more speaking requests. Apparently, true stories of overcoming the classic negative statistics of lower expectations leave a lasting impression. After speaking at more than 50 conferences, schools, and community events, locally and nationally, I still struggled to feel like I was actually making a difference. I wasn't sold on the fact that my little stories really helped. Around this time, I happened to hear an inspirational, yet ego-deflating quote: "Don't try to sell something you don't believe in."

Lacking confidence, guidance, and a sense of purpose, I stopped selling my speaking services for quite some time. Contrary to the smile that was observed by those around me, I failed to believe in myself. Fortunately, unlike many budding young speakers, by the time I reached this turning point in my very slowly growing career, I had already established another career.

Working as a Registered Nurse in emergency departments kept me afloat financially in my early and mid-20's. Entering a health care profession was an economic decision that allowed me to avoid poverty and initiate the end of some of the generational cycles that have plagued much of my immediate and distant family. My health care career also provided me with a great deal of life experiences.

I learned the value of caring and remaining calm in crisis. I learned to accept and empathize with all walks of life. I learned that not everyone thinks the way I do. I learned that I really do not need to be right all the time. Proving my point in any conversation or argument was a very significant downfall of my own. In the past, it has been very embarrassing to not be able to stop myself from over-explaining when I fear that someone might think I did something wrong; no matter how small the issue (this was undoubtedly a side-effect of being labeled a "troubled kid" and other traumatic experiences from my youth). When you are often expected to be the "bad kid" around other "normal" families, you tend to over-explain even when it is not necessary. I learned that I am no better than anyone else and nobody else is any better than me. If someone tries to make me feel like less than them, no matter their perceived professional status, it is usually their own issue. I also learned that many ER nurses have a tendency to be rather intense and unforgiving to young "newbies." This is to be expected to a certain extent, given the truly life or death situations faced on a daily basis. However, the intensity of the interactions between seasoned nurses and those who may be less experienced can often go beyond necessary in this environment. This is a pattern I noticed from having worked in 8 different emergency departments in two states.

Ironically, many interactions with overworked and underpaid nurses often reveal a lack of self-awareness and an attempt to avoid facing the reality of an unhappy life that has likely been compounded by their own trauma. This, of course, is not a blanket statement, and such individuals could easily be identified in nearly any profession. There were also many co-workers whose great helping hearts even facilitated my own growth. I learned, and continue to learn, how to apply these, and many other, key principles to everyday life. These lessons have allowed me to build and maintain successful professional and personal relationships, and most importantly, live a happier and healthier life.

Learning and applying these principles takes a lifestyle of dedication to personal growth. I say "lifestyle" instead of lifetime because this lifestyle can be learned and implemented at any time by anyone who is willing to push themselves mentally, emotionally and yes, even physically. This may contradict the way of thinking that is often referred to as "deferred happiness" in which you must live through a life of dissatisfaction, slave away at a job you hate, and then finally achieve the lifestyle you always dreamed of during the retirement that is inevitably lacking substance. If you never develop into the type of person you want to be before retirement, what makes you think that no longer working in your career field is going to overhaul habits engrained through a lifetime of deferment? You never developed the way of thinking or the habits that facilitates the lifestyle you always dreamed of. The result is that both your current and future life will lack self-care, self-improvement, and true happiness.

Tim Ferris explains in his book The 4 Hour Work Week how society places so many expectations on us to fulfill other people's agendas that we never take initiative to fulfill our own agenda. In-turn, we stop learning, settle for lower expectations, and wonder what we did with our lives. It took me ten years to grasp this concept and have the courage to make my own decisions. I finally accepted that if I placed anything above achieving a lifestyle that facilitates mental, emotional, and physical wellness, I was only telling myself that other people have control of my life and that I was not as important as they are. It does not take a lifetime to develop this lifestyle, it takes determination to be your best and do your best today, not tomorrow.

Even if you were once there but have fallen off the wagon of personal development, a lifestyle dedicated to self-actualization can be recreated through the power of where you place your energy and focus. I have learned that it truly boils down to decisions. Deciding to make a habit of drinking green tea instead of coffee; deciding to set a fitness goal and start working on it instead of saying you're too busy. Deciding to learn something new every week instead of wasting your spare moments playing solitaire on your PC – ahem, excuse me; I mean, Flappy Bird and other mind-numbing games on your smart phone. Once your lifestyle of personal growth is implemented and/or re-inspired, one can sense the emotional growth almost immediately.

A lifestyle of personal growth is something anyone can benefit from, regardless of where you come from or what your beliefs are. However, reaching the point where we actually have that lifestyle can be a little daunting. How do you even get started when there might be so many things you want to change? Here are a couple of tips to climbing that Maslow Hierarchy of Needs and starting to feel self-actualized through doing rather than dreaming:

Stop Comparing Yourself to Others

Do you have that friend that always seems to have it together? Whenever you see them, something new is going on. They've started a Pilate's class and feel AMAZING, or their daughter is the rising star of her soccer league. Their Facebook statuses and pictures always feature them flashing their perfectly straight (of course) smile. Having friends like that can sometimes be discouraging because you might feel that anything you try to change will pale in comparison to what they already have. "They make it look so effortless," you think, "maybe some people are just meant to be self-actualized while others are meant to eat Cheetos on the couch like me." I urge you though to remember the Steven Furtick quote that says, "The reason we struggle with insecurity is because we compare our behind-the-scenes with everyone else's highlight reel."

You don't always know what is going in someone's life. Remember the pesky 16-year-old neighbor from earlier in the book? She could be dealing with a personal trauma or tragedy that you never would've imagined if you didn't take the time to look beyond her mask (of heavy makeup). Instead of getting caught up in surface appearance, it is beneficial to remind yourself that short of following someone around through every moment of their day (which is stalking, and I don't think you should do that), you don't know how "perfect" their life really is. If you ever find you're beating yourself up because you don't compare to someone else, it is good to bear in mind that you see all the mundane details of your own life, but your friend or co-worker is only showing you what they want you to see.

Besides not having all the information about someone's life, keep in mind that everything, is relative. For a moment, imagine you start going to the gym. When you first start out you can curl 15 pounds. Within a month of diligence, you're up to 20, or even 25 pounds. Does that compare to what a bodybuilder or fitness model can curl? No, not even close! But these are professionals who have put way more time into working on your physical strength than you, and have been doing it for much longer. Instead of downplaying your efforts by thinking that you're not as good as someone else, compare your progress from when you started to where you are now. I'm sure you will be pleased with what you find. And if not, keep at it! There is always time to put more effort into personal development. For nutrition and fitness tips from my own journey of reaching my health and wellness goals including before and after photos, visit my blog at www.TravisLloyd.net/blog.

The "One More" Rule

So you've reached the point where you've made a decision to change your life, be it your eating habits, attitude, fitness, etc. But how do you make a decision and stick to it? We already know through many of the abandoned gym memberships from New Year's resolutions that it can be immensely difficult to commit to what you've decided. I think one of the common pitfalls people face is that they get overwhelmed with the big picture goal and abandon it because it seems too scary. When attempting to make or break a habit, I find the "one more" rule to be invaluable.

The "one more" rule is exactly that, one more of anything you're doing. One more day without a cigarette. One more page on your blog entry. One more push-up. What you find is when you do "one more", you discover that that one more thing wasn't as bad as you thought it was. Take the example of quitting smoking. Most smokers will have a morning cigarette. If you keep pushing back the time you have that cigarette, saying to yourself, "I'll wait one more hour", you'll find at the end of that hour, you're still breathing, the sky hasn't fallen, and you haven't had that cigarette. Then you say to yourself, "Okay, I did one hour, how about one more hour?" Breaking down your goals into small steps makes it seem much more attainable than telling yourself, "Okay, I have to quit smoking forever, starting now!"

Make a Plan

This piece of advice may seem antithetical to the "one more" rule, but take my word for it you, need both. Although breaking your lifestyle changes into smaller steps makes it easier to stick to your decisions, you have to have an ultimate end goal in mind. It is helpful if the goal is specific, such as, "I want to lose 20 pounds this year." Yet even having an over-arching ideal you're striving for, for example, "I want to be more physically active" gives you a compass point to refer to.

Having a plan with both short- and long-term goals will focus you when you're feeling aimless or unmotivated. Instead of shrugging when you ask yourself, "Why am I doing this?" you'll actually have an answer to give yourself. "Oh yeah, that's right, I want to be a better person." Having a plan, especially if you write your plan down, keeps you from forgetting what you want to do to change your life, and holds you accountable. No one likes to look at a piece of paper with their plan on it and realize they've gotten off track. Having that plan in the first place helps reduce the likelihood of that happening.

Emotional growth is a sense of freedom and control. An inner peace that allows you to focus on what truly matters and you slowly start to feel like the great person you are meant to be. The little devil on your left shoulder will always be there; but with each small accomplishment, you gain another ounce of confidence, happiness, and freedom. Little things in life start to matter more and you start to be more sensitive to your surroundings. You start to innately learn more and allow life's lessons to teach you. It starts with saying yes when the easiest thing to do is to say no.

This was very difficult for me to learn and apply to my life, which is why it took me until the end of my 20's before I truly understood why I wanted to speak, write, and perform and how it could make a difference. However, if I had never taken action to accept the challenge of speaking for a group of lawyers, I would have never had the courage to continue. I would have never gotten to travel the country speaking, and I most certainly would have never had the dedication to write this book.

CHAPTER 17

FINDING PASSION & PURPOSE

"For the first time, I said yes to taking action and taking control of my happiness..."

Three months after graduating from college, I remember waking up one day feeling a complete lack of purpose. I had spent four and a half years studying to establish a "good" career only to ask myself one perplexing question; "Is this really real life?" Sure, everyone goes through big life changes and has those "feeling lost" moments from time to time. For some reason, though, this seemed to be more than just a "what am I going to do with my life" crisis.

I had much more fun in college when I was too busy to think. A full time load of classes paired with three 8 hour shifts at work and my full time hobby — hanging out in a hip-hop and R&B (rhythm & blues) home recording studio dreaming of being on stage — did wonders for my ability to avoid my emotions. But after graduation, working three 12 hour shifts each week and picking up an extra shift here and there to cover the massive student loan debt left me with approximately three to four days of complete boredom. I quickly came to the long overdue realization that my social skills weren't that great. I did not have a solid network of support, and I was completely clueless on how to live a fulfilling life. To be honest, I probably couldn't have even offered a definition for the term "fulfilling life." Much of that was likely due to delayed psychosocial development resulting from a less than desirable childhood and psychologically traumatizing events. On reflection, I must say part of it was my own fear; fear of the unknown and fear of going outside of my comfort zone. I once saw a random quote image from an unknown author on Facebook that said, "Those who are bored are usually boring." I interpret that quote to mean that we are each in control of our own life, including the activities and relationships that create excitement, or lack there of. At that time, I was definitely lacking excitement and did not understand how to be in charge of the projection of my own life.

Critical Thinking Moment: Do you feel like a boring bachelor? If you do, continue reading for tips on branching out. If you don't, it is likely you know someone who does. Try making a new friend or deepening a friendship by sharing your passion with whoever that person is in your life! It could make all the difference in their world.

I felt a bit of a depression starting to sink in, so I visited my doctor and he wanted to put me on antidepressants. I had been down that path before, though, and the side effects of Buspar and Lexapro seemed worse than fighting through it on my own. So, I did what any boring bachelor would do; I got a six week old puppy named Zeus.

Zeus kept me company and gave me something productive to do. I studied and implemented dominance training and stayed dedicated to consistency in order to have an extremely well behaved dog that could walk without a leash. I think having a dog that minded my directions made me feel more accomplished, even manly, and provided a slight compensation for what I lacked in other departments. I realized how important consistency was, and deep down I think that is when I realized that I wished I would have had more consistency in my younger years.

Boxers have a tendency to gain attention in public places, and Zeus was the epitome of a chiseled boxer who looked mean enough to protect a palace, but was more likely to tuck his tail and lick your nose than attack. Zeus' perfect manners paired with his handsome boxer physique earned him many admirers. My favorite was, of course, the beautiful women who inevitably stopped to pet him.

They always loved his playful demeanor and strong name; Zeus. Unfortunately, the dog and beautiful woman introduction never led to a beautiful woman and human introduction. When a woman seemed to be exactly what I desired, I couldn't quite spit out, "Oh, and I'm Travis. It's nice to meet you, what's your name?" There might have been some insecurities that prevented a personal introduction. Of course, it could have also had something to do with the fact that as a young adult and recent college grad, I had an utterly boring life and lacked basic social skills. I felt like life was just passing me by. Working a stressful job in the ER and training my dog just didn't give me the fulfillment I desired. I couldn't place it at the time, but eventually I would recognize what I desired the most was to be a part of a bigger purpose; to help others. Yet again, the desire to fight for the underdog that initiated in my teenage years working as a residential counselor would shine through.

My friend Joe, a former roommate in the fraternity, was dating a girl named Steph at the time. I had never been very close to Steph, so it was a bit awkward to answer my phone one Spring afternoon and hear her voice. Since all of my friends knew how much of a "ladies man" I was, especially in college, I worked hard to avoid talking to anyone they dated even though I had a strict rule to never date a friend's current or ex-girlfriend. Even good friends would sometimes be suspicious if I talked to their girlfriend due to my previous flaunting of women I dated. Little did I know that this awkward conversation would change the trajectory of my life forever.

I was walking Zeus in the nearby grass field when Steph helped shape the next stage of my life, passion, and career. She said that she remembered hearing about me having once been in foster care. The topic alone was still triggering for me, so I hesitantly asked why she was interested. As she continued I could sense excitement in her voice.

"I was a social work major and I am almost graduated," she said. "In order to get my degree, I have to do internship hours." So I am interning for a foster care program in Des Moines. Our program is growing across the state, and they have started a group in your region. I think that you can really relate to a lot of these kids since you dealt with some tough situations growing up." I was very skeptical, but the sincerity in her voice comforted me. I said yes immediately. *For the first time, I said yes to taking action and taking control of my happiness*, as well as my future.

Saying yes opened a world of opportunities for me. I had thought that I was saying yes to being a volunteer with local foster youth. Within three weeks I found out that my "yes" implied that I would become the new regional facilitator for the state-wide foster youth advisory council. I became immediately passionate about helping these young people understand their behaviors and how to overcome the lower expectations placed by the label "foster kid." I became eager to lead in this organization that facilitated helping these young people find their voice and advocate for community awareness and legislative changes to improve foster care and the child welfare system. I taught the youth as much as I could from my own experiences of struggling with emotional disturbances, unhealthy relationships, and learning to balance both screens. Through this roll I learned as much as I taught.

Little did I know, that within three months my work with this foster youth organization would bring me to Atlanta, Georgia where I had the opportunity to perform one of my hip-hop songs that I had written about my life story. Shortly after, the program director contracted me to create an entire hip-hop and poetry album that would showcase the voices of the foster youth in our program. That year I spent three to six months recording the voices of the youth that we worked with from across the state. Some of them recited poetry and some of them simply talked about their troubles, while other sang or performed rap lyrics. My old friends from the home studio that I spent hours upon hours with as a college student helped me complete the album by providing all of the music and production to turn it into a professional project; it was perfect.

The next 18 months were filled with many more "yes" answers that would push me out of my comfort zone and into my passion. I had the opportunity to perform my music at an annual fundraiser called Reggie's Sleepout that helped raise over $150,000 for homeless youth. This led to the opportunity to co-produce, write and perform voiceovers for radio and TV commercials. Invitations to speak to social work conferences quickly followed, along with my first professionally paid speaking engagement for the foster youth council in Las Vegas, Nevada. These opportunities continued to open more doors, including the opportunity to build a speaking and entertaining business with my friend Dante' from the old in-home studio. That business has since evolved into our own separate businesses. Saying yes to that opportunity and the experiences that came along with our traveling to speak to at-risk youth all across the country prepared me for each step that was to follow. It also taught me many lessons about being open to new cultures and experiences that can and will change your life.

Once you take action and say yes to enough experiences, you will eventually find something you are passionate about, something that you never realized was missing until you found it, or it might even be a hobby that you once abandoned. Any of these is great! But something may still be missing: your friends and support group. For those who still struggle with overcoming past traumas, it is very easy to isolate yourself. It is common to have insecurities and underdeveloped socials skills. This may cause you to feel like you are a loner, or that nobody else understands you. This may be true for you, even if you have a professional job or go to school full time. You are around people, but your interactions may be very superficial. But building a form of support and companionship is one of the biggest steps towards having a happier and healthier life; and it makes enjoying your passions that much easier.

Whether you are introverted or extroverted, we are social animals and, eventually, being alone can have adverse psychological effects such as being fearful of emotional bonds, becoming more self-conscious, and impaired communication skills. There's a reason that solitary confinement is such a grueling punishment: humans are meant to be with other humans. How do you actually go about getting that friendship and support from others to share your passions with you, especially if you are shy or lack social skills? I find that these tips have been useful for me in coming out of my shell:

Strangers are Friends you haven't Met Yet

Remember when I said humans are social animals? Well, that hasn't changed between this paragraph and the last. Imagine that you're talking to a new person and you start doubting yourself or worrying that they don't want to talk to you, relax. You might begin to realize that it's probably not as bad as you're making it out to be, and that everyone wants to make social connections. If you go up and talk to someone out of the blue, some of the time the person may respond uncomfortably. However, much of the time you'll find that the person will be friendly and receptive.

I have made friends through approaching them without being formally introduced. It helps if you're in a location where you are relaxed or waiting for something, such as a coffee shop, waiting for the bus, or a dog park. Generally, if someone is walking quickly down the street, they're not looking to stop and chat. If someone is already in a less tense state, say they're enjoying their cappuccino in a comfy chair at the local coffee shop, they are much more receptive to unexpected social contact.

This isn't to say that you won't face rejection occasionally; to be realistic, it's the law of averages. Sometimes your attempt to interact will be met with discomfort or hostility because the other person is having a bad day. Don't take it personally! Don't trouble yourself with the ones who say no. Instead, focus on the people who say yes.

You won't Connect with Everyone

So, you're talking to a human being. Good for you! You're on the path to gaining a new friend. But what if things don't seem to be flowing? They like PC gaming, you haven't played a video game since Atari; they only speak with one syllable words, making conversation very difficult to keep afloat while you like to engage in full and meaningful conversations. Sometimes you'll meet someone, and it doesn't quit click. Don't force it, there is nothing wrong with you, sometimes you just don't click with a person.

You can't always connect. If we were meant to have a profound connection with everyone around the world, that would be absurd!

It would be impossible to maintain such an elaborate network of meaningful connections. If you're talking to someone you don't find that interesting or you don't have much in common with, try to let it go and move on rather than blaming yourself for being "boring" or "socially awkward." Everyone is boring to someone; it's all dependent on what your interests and core values are. If this happens, it is best to not agonize over the experience, but to move on instead. Save your energy for people whom you are going to truly cherish and find enriching in your life. Spending your valuable time on pretending to like certain things for someone else's sake, or even keeping contact with another because you want to be nice isn't doing yourself, or the other person any favors.

Find community clubs or online forums about your interest or passion. Not only will it increase the likelihood that you'll find someone you get along with, but it can also be motivation to keep going with your passion. If you're in an online forum for writers, and there are users expecting to read one of your poems because you said you would have it up by Monday, it keeps you accountable and forces you to not get too distracted with life's many worries, but to take the time for yourself to pursue what you love the most. One of the things that I talk about in my health, wellness, and fitness report is connecting with other likeminded individuals using social media groups and hashtags. I have met good friends through discussions initiated in the comment section of Facebook and Instagram photos. There is a page in the back of this book that tells you how to receive a free copy of this report.

Remember, if it doesn't quite feel right, then it probably isn't worth your time. Focus on what makes you happy and give positive vibes to everyone possible. Spreading hope and passion to others will continue to keep you active and engaged in life rather than watching life pass you by.

EPILOGUE

To some of you, the stories and lessons you have read are brand new topics and ideas; to others, they may be good reminders of lessons once learned, but not practiced often enough. Each of you, however, may be in the same boat of wondering, "What now? What do I do with these stories?" It is very easy to walk away inspired, yet never applying lessons to your life.

One thing that I've learned is that every time I invest my time and energy in getting to know someone else's story, I get to make a decision: to walk away inspired or to embrace a new viewpoint and create new habits, try new things, and push the limit. Personally, I prefer to push the limit; push it just far enough to test my comfort zone and make sure my spirit is still alive!

My hope is that exposing my inner thoughts, fears and desires was not done in vain; that at least one person, maybe you, walks away knowing that it is possible to simply just exist and accept yourself for who you are. What I shared was not just to offer inspiration and hope, but to also stimulate the internal motivation to dig deep inside of your heart, mind, and spirit to overcome. Not just to continue surviving each mundane day, but to actively seek out ways to make a difference in the lives of your friends, family members, schoolmates and co-workers. To invest in developing meaningful relationships and welcome the opportunities that inspires your passions. To always view your dreams as possible, but not just to see the possibilities; to set goals and small actionable steps that allow you to see progress over time as your dreams evolve into reality. To say yes when at one time you would have said no. And to develop and maintain a lifestyle that allows you to be happier, healthier, and more successful - however you define success.

I hope that you find meaning in your relationships and fill your days with the opportunities and people who make you happy. Learning to understand and appreciate your past journey, and the journeys of those around you, helps you to accept what was and what now is. Accepting it is one step towards overcoming and no longer being stuck in survival mode.

Something that I've wanted to impress upon you throughout the book is that human experience is subjective; what is traumatic for one person may not be traumatic for another. Indeed, everyone deals with stress and trauma a little differently. On one hand, this can be a liberating experience. Once you get it out of your head that there is no right way to feel, hopefully you can get over any shame or guilt and express what you need to express to a trusted loved one or professional. On the other hand, this can be a scary thought. If you are experiencing something in a unique way, how is anyone supposed to truly understand what you're going through? Is it possible to seek help, or am I left out in the dark alone? Well, you should know from reading this book that the answer to the last question is a resounding yes! You may experience an event in a slightly different way than someone else, but that doesn't mean the empathy and support of others and the soul-searching you do on your own is a lost cause. Actually, it can and should be the primary source of your personal development. Input from outside sources should guide, not replace your internal work. For those of you who are just beginning or in the process of overcoming, here are a couple main lessons I hope you give yourself time to reflect on.

You don't have to do this alone. I've mentioned throughout the book the importance of having a support group, and how sharing your story, while scary, can be an essential part of healing. You will feel vulnerable; bringing up painful events of your past will probably cause you to feel some of the feelings you felt long ago, and that is an unpleasant process. It may be difficult to even remember everything because your mind has tried to suppress it. Yet, know that in bringing the skeletons out of the closet, you can evict them from your house. You can only bottle things up for so long before they surface. Your trauma is a time-bomb, and the best way to diffuse it is to try to come to terms with what has happened and find a way to understand the trauma without becoming consumed by your own pain.

Always recognize and respect your needs, be they physical or mental. Stress can affect the body in weird ways, causing psychosomatic symptoms, or actually contributing to the development of heart disease or cancer. Your mind and body have a connection, and if you are not taking care of one, the other will be adversely affected. Get out of survival mode and try to take some time to reflect rather than trying to merely survive moment to moment, day to day. Work diligently to keep your body healthy, eat well, and get enough sleep. Also important is the practice of not relying too heavily on drugs (prescription or illegal) or alcohol. These temporary fixes will cause additional problems on top of whatever problems you might already have. Show yourself respect by taking care of yourself, and in doing so, you will trust yourself and your gut more (and this will keep you out of trouble).

It is important to think long- and short-term. We need those lofty end goals to remind us why we are working so hard, but sometimes they can seem so far away that we feel discouraged and hopeless. Those short-term goals of taking it one little step at a time really add up. Eventually those baby steps cover a lot of ground. An old friend of mine named Chuck was the producer in the home studio that I spent a lot of time in during my college years. When he saw me struggling, he would simply say, "Baby steps to victory." You will be amazed at the progress you can see over time if you stay focused and don't get too caught up in thinking what you're doing is "impossible."

Be patient and have faith. You may have experienced trauma and abuse over years and years; this is not going to be something you can overcome in a day. Even if it was one event, there is no telling how much healing time there may be; it is different for everyone. For a sexual assault victim, one minute of violation could take one year or many years to recover. Trauma is confusing; some, such as Dori Laub, believe that at the heart of trauma is absence, a complete lack of understanding. Unraveling your thoughts and feelings may be tough, but know that with faith in yourself and a commitment to being patient, you can heal.

Looking at my own story is proof that you can take negative experiences from your past and incorporate them into your identity without becoming defined by them. My past will always be a part of who I am, and it has influenced countless decisions in my teenage and adult life that I may not have made if I had had a different childhood. Ultimately, I won't know. All I can do is work through my past and look towards the future. And the future, to me, seems very bright indeed. Even if the road towards overcoming your own emotional trauma seems dark and deep, know that there is respite along the way, and that all your efforts will be worth it.

ACKNOWLEDGEMENTS

A lthough beginning this journey as a first time author was quite the challenge, many people joined by my side to offer support and encouragement along the way. To every person who left a message on my social media pages or through my web site, thank you! Your comments helped me through several sleepless nights with just my keyboard and my dog, Zeus.

A few specific individuals played key roles in this book becoming a reality. I am proud to call each of them friends.

Dr. Chris Downs

I have known Chris for many years. I met him just as I was beginning my journey of becoming a professional speaker. He was a "big wig" for an agency that organized a national foster care conference that I was attending in 2007. Chris later became a good friend and colleague who I can call on for all kinds of things. At times when I felt down about my progress or performance, he has always been there with encouragement and wise words that propelled me through each struggle. I now have the honor of being an Associate in his consulting firm, The Downs Group, LLC. Chris has a passion for improving services to and outcomes for older youth in out-of-home care at the local, state-wide and national level. I encourage you to check out his company at www.DownsConsultingGroup.com.

Dr. Gregory Keck

You will hear how I met Greg as you read through the stories in the book, so I won't ruin it for you here. However, I will share that Greg and I also connected at the beginning of my speaking career, and he has always been a consistent voice of encouragement. When I first had the dream of writing a book, he told me that he would help me in any way possible, including contributing material that supported my views and stories. It is not very often that you meet someone who is willing to put their neck out for you before you have even proven yourself. This is the reason why I had the courage to start writing; I knew he had my back. Four years later, I finally made good on my dream and wrote a book; and Greg kept his word in contributions. He is also the founding psychologist of the Attachment and Bonding Center of Ohio where, for multiple decades, they have provided truly effective trauma informed care practices. Learn more at www.ABCofOhio.net.

Christy Meyer, Retired Therapist

I have only known Christy a short time, but in this short time, she has left a lasting impression as a true friend. Later in the book, I will share about Christy and her amazing approach to loving those who many would say are unlovable; so, again, I won't ruin the surprise. I will, however, share with you that during the writing process, Christy selflessly offered her time and ideas to ensure that this book reflects not just my story, but key learning points that we both find imperative to helping others live happier, healthier, and more successful lives. Even as a retiree, she continues to serve as a crisis worker and provides trainings on trauma informed care practices for foster parents.

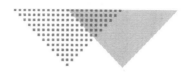

ABOUT THE AUTHOR

Travis Lloyd is a motivational speaker, author, trainer, and consultant with a background as a health care professional and adjunct professor. He is known to share stories of overcoming and inspiring others through real life stories, poetry, and song. As a former hopeless youth who feared his lifestyle would lead to prison, Travis began seeking to discover how to live a life of passion and purpose.

At the age of 23, Travis found what he was seeking for and dedicated the next seven years of his life to gaining the experience and developing the skill necessary to help others do the same. He enjoys speaking, emceeing, and performing for both youth and adult audiences. His past venues range from middle and high schools to universities, juvenile justice, child welfare, and corporate conferences.

Having experienced and overcome foster homes, homeless shelters, and a stay in an adolescent mental health unit enables Travis to offer hope, not only to audiences across the country, but to his own community. Travis previously served as a Mental Health Mobile Crisis Worker, and still occasionally serves as an Adjunct Professor and licensed emergency nurse in a pediatric hospital.

Travis is a board member of Foster Care Alumni Of America, VP of the Our Fields Of Hope Foundation, Google Certified contributor of Social Work Helper Magazine, and Foster Focus Magazine, co-author of Fostering Hope For America, and author of *Overcoming Emotional Trauma: Life Beyond Survival Mode.*

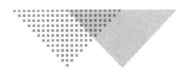

CONNECT WITH TRAVIS

Having supportive mentors and developing a network of like-minded individuals is the one and only thing that kept my dreams alive and allowed me to push through any insecurities to find a happier life. If you want to chat about any of the topics in this book I invite you to write me at Travis@TravisLloyd.net.

Here's a few other ways to reach me:
www.Facebook.com/TravisLloydSpeaks
www.Instagram.com/TravisLloydSpeaks
www.Twitter.com/TravisLloyd

Prefer a professional connection?
www.linkedin.com/in/travislloydspeaks/

www.TravisLloyd.net

DISCUSSIONS & MORE INFO

Thinking of going deeper? Find more information and be updated when new materials and informational videos on overcoming are made available. Simply submit your email address at www.OvercomingEmotionalTrauma.com and we'll let you know!

REFERENCES

Casey Family Programs. Foster Care By The Numbers. 2011.
PDF file. 01 Sept. 2014.
http://www.casey.org/media/MediaKit_osterCareByTheNumbers.pdf

Montgomery, John. Survival Mode and Evolutionary Mismatch.
Psychology Today, 6 December.
2012. Web. 18 August 2014. Web.
http://www.psychologytoday.com/blog/the-embodied-
mind/201212/survival-mode-and-evolutionary-mismatch.

Pecora, P. J., Kessler, R. C., Williams, J., Downs, A C., English,
D. J., White, J., & O'Brien, K.
(2010) What Works in Foster Care? New York: Oxford
University Press. Page 109.AlumniStudies_NW_Report_FR.pdf

FURTHER READING

Bray, Oliver and Bray, Peter, eds. *Voicing Trauma and Truth.* Oxford: Inter-Disciplinary Press, 2013.

Ferris, Timothy. *The 4-Hour Work Week.* New York: Crown Publishing Group, 2009.

Henke, Suzette. *Shattered Subjects: Trauma and Testimony in Women's Life-Writing.* New York: Palgrave Macmillan, 2000.

Levine, Amir, Heller, Rachel S.F. Attached: *The New Science of Adult Attachment and How It Can Help You Find - and Keep - Love.* New York: Penguin Group, 2010.

Tolle, Echart. A New Earth: *Awakening to Your Life's Purpose.* New York: Penguin Group, 2006..

Riordan, Richard J. "Scriptotherapy: Therapeutic Writing as a Counseling Adjunct." *Journal of Counseling and Development.* 74.3. (1996): 263-269. Web. 01 Sept. 2014. http://connection.ebscohost.com/c/articles/9602262357scriptotherapy-therapeutic-writing-as-counseling-adjunct

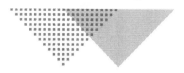

FREE

If you are ready to take the next step in living happier, healthier and being more successful in life and relationships, *this is my gift to you.*

<u>Follow the instructions below</u> to receive 1 (one) free copy of my health, wellness, and fitness report The Body You Want, The Lifestyle You Need.

The information in this report gives you all of the basic tips and advice that it took for me to get fit mentally, emotionally, and physically.

This report outlines:

· How To Get Started
· Diet Myths & Tips
· 5 Statements That Create A Mindset Shift
· 3 Common Exercise Misperceptions
· How I Stay Motivated
· Workout Samples (that I used to get started)

INSTRUCTIONS

1. Take a photo of you holding this book and either smiling or making a goofy face.
2. Post this photo on Facebook, Twitter, Instagram, or LinkedIN and use the hashtag #MyTraumaTalks.
3. Send me an email at Travis@TravisLloyd.net with the subject: I'm Ready! Be sure to tell me where you posted the photo so I can see it!
4. I will write you back personally to thank you and provide you with your free gift!

24889716R00109

Made in the USA
Middletown, DE
10 October 2015